A HAT FULL OF MIRACLES

Lottie Gillmore

A Hat Full of Miracles

Lottie Gillmore

508 West 26th Street KEARNEY, NE 68848
402-819-3224
info@medialiteraryexcellence.com

This Cherished, Little Book IsDedicated

With Sincere Appreciation,

and Loving Honour

To The World's Maker,

Creator and Miracle Worker Our Father,

Daddy, In HeavenJesus, GOD,

His Son And

His Precious Holy Ghost,

Counselor Whom as,

Three in One Lead, Guide and, Heal Us,

His Children

Table of Contents

A Hat Full of Miracles

Stories By

Believers of

Medicine Hat, Alberta, Canada

Miracle 1

Book Number 4 - A Hat Full of Miracles

Hello, from Medicine Hat, Alberta, Canada. My name is Elizabeth Storres and I would like to tell you remarkable miracle stories that have taken place within the lives and hearts' of the people in this fine city.

Many citizens here in the "Hat" are believers in Christ the King, Our Father in Heaven and the Holy Spirit. I would like to share with you, many miracles that these Believers have come forward to tell and share, while in the process to praise our Living God, The HolyTrinity.

This book of miracle's, was started on December 19, 2008, about 4:00 o'clock p.m. in the afternoon while I was driving home from my day-time employment. For twelve years now, I have been writing Christian poetry and children's stories.

On this afternoon, I was driving home alone, talking to and singing praises unto the Lord, Jesus. About a year and one-half earlier, I had felt very strongly to write my testimony of Jesus saving my life from uncountable tragedies and turbulences.

I had almost completely finished my novel manuscript and as I was nearing my home, singing and praying, I all of sudden felt compelled to ask Jesus if I had another book to write and if I did, what was it?

Question stated, with praise on my lips, I continued to drive home while worshipping GOD.

Nothing seemed different. My husband and I had supper. I then worked on the last three pages of my Christian novel and soon it was bedtime. My husband went to bed but for some reason, I was not tired so I resorted to watching some television, ate a snack and checked my e-mails.

After hours of restlessness, I returned to bed, but only to lay beside my sleeping husband, wide awake. A couple more hours passed, with me up and down, and then I was on the move again. I couldn't stay laying down any longer. I got up and just sat quietly with a small light on in the living room. All was quiet and peaceful. The time just ticked away. The clock was reaching 4:30 a.m. and still I couldn't sleep.

Then in a single moment, I heard in my spirit a gentle statement from the Holy Spirit. His words were clear and precise. Without any hesitation He said: "Write a book of peoples personal testimonies of miracles in Medicine Hat".

With wonderment filling my being, I felt God's Holy Presence. I sat there in awe and gratefulness. I had asked GOD's direction for me and again Jesus was Faithfull and answered me. Praise GOD, our Heavenly Father! With excitement gripping me, I almost immediately tried to name the book of miracles. I sat there for about 30 minutes trying out different titles, to a no good conclusion.

Soon it was 5:00 o'clock a.m. and my dear husband of eighteen years, also got up for the day. Him barely awake and up, I started sharing with him of my "GOD" encounter. After sharing with him a few unsettled titles, I started to walk into the kitchen. But as I turned to leave him, Randall stopped me by saying: "What about this title?" Then without hesitation he quoted: "A Hat Full of Miracles." I stopped in my tracks and knew without a doubt that this title was also "GOD given" and just like the title for my personal Christian novel, Randall, again was instrumental in relaying GOD's wishes for this book's title also.

Praise the Lord! GOD had given me the books to write and had given Randall, my loving husband, the names for those books. Thank you, Precious Holy Spirit!!

The very next week, I pursued my mission. I prayed, listened and asked the Holy Spirit for guidance.

As the next few weeks unfolded, it was clear that GOD the Father was opening church doors and people's hearts around our fine city. Priests and Pastors throughout numerous denominations, that were Holy Trinity Believing Churches, welcomed the news of a Believers testimonial book. Church bulletins greeted congregations throughout Medicine Hat, with news of how to share their stories.

By GOD's Holy Grace, this book has been compiled and together as Believers in Christianity, the Love of Jesus Christ, our Wonder-filled Heavenly Father and His precious, Gentle Holy Spirit, come together, as His people stand strongly united in praise!

Thank you, to all who stand together at the foot of the cross, while revisiting GOD's Holy Hand in miraculous action. Find your favorite, comfy chair, curl up with your feet up and let the Love of Jesus wash over your heart, mind, body and soul, as you read about many people around you.

May you each be touched by GOD's unending Mercy and Love as each Believer retells history in this book, as they perceive it.

May those of you reading these pages of Holy testimonies, also be washed with the possibilities of hearing from The Holy Spirit, as He knocks gently, as a Gentleman, on your heart's door. If you don't know Jesus Christ as your personal Savior yet, now possibly is your special time in history, to ask Him in. Jesus loves you so much that He went to the cross to die for your sins and on the third day, rose again. He now sits at the right hand of Father GOD Almighty, while intervening for every person that comes to Him in faith. When we come to GOD and ask sincerely for forgiveness in Jesus Name, GOD is faithful and forgives us. Jesus washes our tarnished, sinful souls white as snow and our names are written in the Book of Lambs.

Mostoutcomes in our daily lives, we are notin control of, even if we think we are. But by asking Jesus, of the universe into our hearts, we can choose "life", now and here-after.

GOD bless each one of you richly, as you enjoy and watch GOD do miraclesin your life!

Miracle 2

Hurricane Hazel

It had to be the darkest night of my life. The night that we lived through, Hurricane Hazel, was a nightmare that we will never forget, as we drove right into that storm.

It was October 15, 1954, my late husband Harvey Guindon, me, Anita and our daughter Linda, who at the time was four months old, were getting ready to go on a trip with Gerry and Hilda Belanger. I had not been listening to the radio, so therefore didn't hear about any severe weather warning for the eastern Ontario area. It had been raining all week around Toronto and surrounding areas, and by Friday the wind was getting stronger all the time.

We left Cornwall, Ontario in mid-afternoon around two. We were on our way to visit Harvey's sister and her family in Fort Erie. We stopped in Kingston for supper.

By then the wind had risen to 80 miles per hour. Along the highwayswere a lot of broken trees with some fallen trees blocking highways two andfour.

Trees five feet in diameter had been toppled by the winds. Many places had power failures. Telephone lines were down in a lot of places. Many Ontario Provincial Police, who were on duty on the highways, were advising motorist that they were traveling at their own risk. By the time we reached Toronto, the winds were at 130 miles per hour. Hurricane Hazel had struck.

Hurricane Hazel was born near the Island of Grenada on October 5, 1954. On October 6, 7, and 8th, Hazel moved slowly west, gathering strength as it moved towards the coast of Venezuela. On October 9, Hazel headed north. On October 10 and 11, Hazel was heading north by northeast towards Haiti. On October 12, Hazel hit the southern peninsula of Haiti with vicious force with winds of 115 miles per hour. On October 13, Hazel began moving toward the Bahamas picking up more speed and heading for Florida.

On October 14, Hazel missed Florida by 300 miles, but was threatening the coast of South Carolina. October 15, at 8 a.m. Hazel was nearing South Carolina with winds at 120 miles per hour, with tides as high as 17 feet. October 15, at 6:30 p.m., Hazel hit the Washington area. By 7 p.m., Hazel was heading north through Maryland, Delaware, Pennsylvania and New York State.

At 11 p.m., October 15, 1954, Hazel was heading out over Lake Ontario. Toronto was not prepared for Hurricane Hazel. In Brampton, Ontario, 8 inches of rain fell in a forty-eight hour period.

For the firemen, policemen, newspapermen, navy men and all kinds of volunteers, it was the stormiest and wildest nightmare they had ever seen when this horrible, Hurricane Hazel, struck. Five volunteer firemen lost their lives in the course of duty while their fire truck fell into the Humber River, crushing it into a shapeless hunk of metal. A thousand stories can be told of incidents and events concerning Hurricane Hazel.

The winds were so strong that it lifted a barn up in the air and set it back down nearby without harming the five cows that were in it. The Grand River rose 10 inches in twenty minutes. There were 27 firemen who spent all night rescuing marooned residents.

A story was told how a man rescued twenty-seven cats and fourteen dogs. In Woodbridge, twenty mobile homes were swept downriver. It was a night of terror, horror and destruction. It was a night never to be forgotten by some Ontario residents. It was a night of deaths and a night of miracles.

Nancy Thorpe, a four-month old baby was left an orphan to the storm. Her parents called firemen to come and rescue baby Nancy. The Thorpe's had lived through floods before and did not expect danger. But they wanted their baby to have extra care in case of danger. The firemen picked her up with a small suitcase full of formula.

The truck they were driving got marooned as there was six feet of water around them after they had rescued two people on top of marooned cars. They just had to wait for help. Finally somebody with a cedar strip boat rescued them and took them atop of the roof of a cement blockhouse. The damage and sight of Hurricane Hazel was just ghostly. Four homes in the area where baby Nancy was rescued from, were all under water. Baby Nancy lost her parents, a 2-year-old brother and her grandmother. After spending all night on top of a house, baby Nancy and 31 other people and three dogs all soaked and shivering, were all rescued by a front-end loader. Baby Nancy was handed over to the Red Cross. She slept most of the night but was fed often, as she was premature. Nancy's mother had wrapped her up warmly as she was held by a 16-year-old girl all night. It was a miracle baby Nancy survived.

Raymore Drive was a sheet that would never be seen again as it disappeared during Hurricane Hazel. An elderly couple of 63 years of age spent the night on top of the roof of their house, in light clothing with their dog, until a helicopter saved them. Not everyone was that lucky, as 36 people lost their lives who were residents of Raymore Drive. There were 60 families that were left homeless and 1200 feet of the sheet was gone. Weary rescue workers had their headquarters at a small church, not far from Raymore Drive, which is where they took all of the survivors. Most of them were in shock as it was too much for them to comprehend. After dealing with death and destruction, Hurricane Hazel died over James Bay. It took a lot of volunteer worker's to clean up the aftermath. Such as the Police, the Military, boy scouts, the Red Cross, CNIB, the Salvation Army, and the Fire Department. A morgue was setup on the second floor of the old Fire Department, on Dundas Street.

Most people had no chance of surviving as they were still in their pajamas. These organizations did magnificent work in cleaning up after Hurricane Hazel.

It's amazing how your body can keepon going without any sleep at a time likethis. Mr. Sanderson worked for thirty-sixhours trying to restore power, without any sleep and Bill Swann who was an engineer, worked seventy-two hours without sleep. After their jobs were done their boss took them to a very elegant restaurant, in their dirty foul-smelling coveralls. I'm sure they would have been thrown out of that place at any other time. But after working hard the way they did they surely deserved a hot meal.

Some of the girls that worked for Bell Telephone stayed at the office for one week working long hours and double shifts. Death took its toll as eighty-one people lost their lives during Hurricane Hazel and three thousand were left homeless.

Canada opened their hearts with large amounts of donations coming in, from six to fifteen bags of mail arriving three times a day. Some checks, as high as $100,000 were coming in and also a check for $10,000, came from overseas.

In the Humber Valley area where Hurricane Hazel ripped through, leaving a terrible mess, there is today one of the most picturesque and beautiful parks in the entire province of Ontario. Someday I'm hoping to go to Toronto and see that Park. Once there I know it will bring tears to my eyes as I think back forty years ago, on October 15, 1954. While holding my daughter Linda, of four months old and praying to God all the way from Toronto to Fort Crie, we prayed that we would all survive. God in His Mercy did answer us and kept us alive.

At one point, the water on the highway was above the wheels of our car. That's when I was the most scared. In my mind I thought that we were all going to die, in this storm of Hurricane Hazel, during the most destructing storm I have ever witnessed. To think that I'm able to recall the night of October 15,

1954 is unbelievable. I can remember every detail as if it were yesterday. I can remember telling friends and relatives how a bridge collapsed and was washed away one hour after we had passed over it. I believe it was the Humber Bridge. It took us twelve hours to drive from Cornwall, Ontario to Fort Crie, Ontario, which normally would have taken half that time. My late husband's sister thought that we had to be out of our mind to have traveled during such a storm. I fed my daughter then put her to bed. I had a bowl of soup and after talking to my sister-in-law for half an hour, I decided to go to bed, as I was emotionally exhausted. My late husband Harvey stayed up all night visiting with his sister. Three days later we returned back to Cornwall by train and the other couple stayed one week. I, Anita, will always be eternally grateful to the Lord, for having saved our lives!

Miracle Event by,

Anita Guindon, Seamstress

Miracle 3

The Plague in Lisbon
The City Saved By His Holy Name

A devastating plague broke out in Lisbon in 1432. All who could do so fled in terror from the city and thus carried the plague to every corner of the entire country of Portugal.

Thousands of men, women and children of all classes were swept away by the cruel sickness. So virulent was the epidemic that men died everywhere, at table, in the street, in their houses, in the shops, in the marketplaces, in the churches. To use the words of historians, it flashed like lightning from man to man, or from a coat, a hat or any garment that had been used by the plague-stricken. Priest, doctors and nurses were carried off in such numbers that the bodies of many lay un buried in the streets, so that the dogs licked up the blood and ate the flesh of the dead, becoming as a result themselves infected with the dread disease and spreading it still more widely among the unfortunate people.

Among those who assisted the dying with unflagging zeal was a venerable bishop, Monastery of St. Dominic. This holy man, seeing that the epidemic, far from diminishing, grew every day in intensity and despairing of human help, urged the unhappy people to call on the Holy Name of Jesus. He was seen wherever the disease was fiercest, urging, imploring the sick and the dying, as well as those who had not as yet been stricken down, to repeat, "Jesus, Jesus." "Write it on card," he said, "and keep those cards on your persons; place them at night under your pillows; place them on your doors; but above all, constantly invoke with your lips and in your hearts this most powerful Name.

He went about as an angel of peace filling the sick and the dying with courage and confidence. The poor sufferers felt within them a new life and calling on Jesus, they wore the cards on their breasts or carried them in their pockets.

Then summoning them to the great Church of St. Dominic, he once more spoke to them of the power of the Nameof Jesus and blessed water in the same Holy Name, ordering all the people to sprinkle themselves with it and sprinkle it on the faces of the sick and dying.

Wonder of wonders! The sick got well, the dying arose from their agonies, the plague ceased and the city was delivered in a few days from the most awful scourge that had ever visited it.

The news spread to the whole country and all began, with one accord, to callon the Name of Jesus. In an incredibly short time all Portugal was freed from the dread sickness.

The grateful people, mindful of the marvels they had witnessed, continued their love and confidence in the Name of our Saviour, so that in all their troubles, in all danger, when evils of any kind threatened them, they invoked the Name of Jesus. Confraternities were formed in the churches, processions of the Holy Name were made monthly, altars were raised in honor of this blessed name, so that the greatest curse that had ever fallen on the country was transformed into the greatest blessing.

For long centuries this great confidence in the Name of Jesus continued in Portugal and thence spread to Spain, to France and to the whole world.

Miracle Story sent in by: Wilbert Z

Miracle 4

Jesus Visits
The Blessed Sacraments

I was born in a little town called Fox Valley. I was born into a "Jesus" believing Christian Catholic home of thirteen children plus mom and dad. Our parent's faithfully took us regularly to Mass. I received Holy Communion all of my life. I was married later in the city of Medicine Hat, Alberta, where we have lived many, many years. Now I would like to share a miracle that is very dear to me.

Every weekday morning, Monday through Friday, for many years I have attended Eucharistic Mass at St. Joeseph's Home in our fair city. For the last five years or so, I have been blessed personally, to witness the personal image of Jesus, regularly each Friday morning as the Blessed Sacrament is placed on the Monstrance, by the Priest.

I see Jesus' presence, standing behind the table with the Blessed Sacraments in front of Him.

I see His presence only when the Blessed Sacrament is put out. During the receiving of the Blessed Sacrament, I only know He is present, I don't see His Image anymore at this service. But faithfully, Friday after Friday, my Precious Savior returns to our Blessed Sacrament for me to witness. I thank God for His Devine Presence.

Miracle Story by:

M. B.

Mother, Grandmother and
Great Grandmother

Of six

Miracle 5

The Eucharistic Miracle of Lanciano, Italy

In the city of Lanciano, around the year 700 of Our Lord there was a monk who, although learned in the sciences of the world, was ignorant in those of God, and therefore not strong in his faith. He was plagued by a doubt as to whether the consecrated Host was truly the Body of Christ, and the consecrated wine truly His Blood.

He was a person dedicated more to science than to wisdom, interested more in the world than in the Absolute, trusting more in reason than in contemplation. We can recognize in him a person of our own times: he resembles each of us to an extraordinary degree.

However, he constantly prayed that God would take this wound from his heart, and divine grace did not abandon him, because the almighty God, Father of mercy and consolation, was pleased to raise him up from the depths of his darkness and to grant him that same grace that he had shown to the Apostle St. Thomas.

One morning, as he was celebrating Mass, after he had already said the most holy words of consecration ("This is My Body..., This is My Blood...."), as Jesus had taught it to his Apostles, his doubts and errors weighed upon him more heavily than ever. By a most singular and marvelous favour then, he saw the Bread changed into Flesh and then wine into Blood.

Frightened and confused by so great and so stupendous a Miracle, he stood quite a while as if transported in a divine ecstasy; but eventually, his fear gave way to the spiritual happiness that filled his soul, and he turned his joyful yet tearful face to those around him, exclaiming, "...Behold the Flesh and the Blood of our Most Beloved Christ."

At those words, the bystanders ran with devout haste to the altar and, completely terrified, began, not without copious tears, to cry for mercy. The faithful, who, having become direct witnesses themselves, spread the news throughout the city.

Today, twelve centuries after the miraculous occurrence, the Holy Relics have remained practically intact. Upon a superficial examination, the Host of Flesh, which is still in one piece and has retained the dimensions of the original "Large Host", has a fibrous appearance and a brown color, which becomes light-reddish if a person places a light in the back of the Ostensorium.

The Blood, contained in the chalice, has an earthy color, inclined toward the yellow of ocher, and consists of five coagulated globules. Each of the parts is uneven in shape and size, and when weighed together, the total weight is equal to that of each piece.

The actual spot of the Miracle is located beneath the present-day Church of St. Francis. The Miracle Itself is preserved in the second tabernacle, which is found in the middle of the high altar. The Host, now changed to Flesh, is contained in a silver Monstrance. The wine, now changed to Blood, is contained in a crystal chalice.

Official Position of the Catholic Church

Local Church and Vatican officials have authenticated the Holy Relics on many occasions since the middle ages. In 1672, Pope Clement X declared the altar of the Eucharistic Miracle a privileged altar on all Mondays of the year. In 1887, the Archbishop of Lanciano obtained from Pope Leo XIII a plenary indulgence in perpetuity to those who visit the Church of the Miracle during the eight days preceding the annual feast day, which falls on the last Sunday in October.

Scientific Studies

A rigorous scientific analysis was performed in 1970-71 by Professor Dr. Odorardo Linoli, University Professor at large in anatomy and pathological histology and in chemistry and clinical microscopy, Head Physician of the United Hospitals of Arezzo. Prof. Linoli was assisted by Prof. Dr. Ruggero Bertelli, a Professor Emeritus of anatomy at the University of Sienna.

The research done on the fragmentsof the Blood and the Flesh yielded the following results:

. The Blood of the Eucharistic Miracle is real blood and the Flesh is real flesh.

. The Flesh consists of the muscular tissue of the heart.

. The Blood and the Flesh belong to the human species.

. The blood type is identical in the Blood and in the Flesh.

. The proteins in the Blood are in the

same proportions as those found in normal fresh blood.

. There is no trace whatsoever of any materials or agents used for preservationof flesh or blood.

Science, when called to testify, has confirmed what we have believed in Faith and what the Catholic Church as taught for the last 2,000 years; echoing the words of Christ, "My flesh is real food; my blood is real drink. Whoever eats my flesh and drinks my blood dwell continually in my and I dwell in him." (John 6:55-56)

Miracle Story sent in by: Wilbert Zinger

Miracle 6

Double Miracle

I was saved when I was 30 years old but fell from God's grace for many years. About five years ago, way up on a mountain far from any church, God and I again became one. My mate had mental problems and I went to God. It felt so wonderful to talk and show him glory.

One night my mate thought that people were coming to kill him so we put all the furniture against the windows and doors. He had five rifles and one short gun. He had me lying on the floor with a couch in front of me. He kept circling the room with a weapon. They were all in reach and I was to reload them when the time came. I laid there and kept saying good overcomes evil over and over again. I wasn't frightened at all, as I kept repeating the words, "Good over comes evil." I felt complete shield surround me and I knew that God had surrounded me with this shield and I could not be harmed.

I could feel the presence of the Almighty, so strong, it was the most joyous feeling I have ever had. I knew I was safe. This paranoia with my mate had been going on for a couple years but was getting worse all the time.

I knew my Mom need me home in her town, as she was sick and was 89 years old. I was however 1400 miles away and could not find a way to get out of my sour situation to come to her.

About two weeks after the gun incident my mate came to my bedroom about 9:30 p.m. and grabbed me. He dragged me down the hallway. At the front door he threw a coat and my boots at me as I asked what are you doing. He just said: "Come quickly. I must save you."

It was November 29 and there was a lot of snow where we were. He dragged me out of the house and across the road. Then he threw me in the snow. As I fell,

I saw headlights coming up the road. It was very dark out. He was sitting on my back and had my head pushed in the snow. The truck was driving slowly and I heard the women say to the man: "Stop there is something in the ditch!" The man driving didn't want to stop but the woman insisted! He rolled down his window and asked if everything was alright and my mate said: "Yes."

I was able to raise my head and I said: "NO, it wasn't alright!"

They both jumped out of the truck and as they did my mate got off of me. They helped me up into their truck. They had been grocery shopping which they never before had done at night time before. Mountain people were in their homes when darkness came and this couple mostly did the same.

My Precious God had them pass by just at that time. Praise The Lord! I was in the truck with them and my mate was in the back of the truck. The people first had to go ome and drop off their groceries. Then they took me to the police station. My mate was still in the box of the truck. The poor man was looking wild and making no sense at all.

When we got to the police station, he saw where we were and jumped out of the truck's box and ran in the bushes. We went into the police station. To this day I don't know what my neighbors said to the police but a couple of the Officers ran out and in a short time found my mate. They took him to the hospital where he was admitted to the mental ward.

I was driven home. The next day one of the neighbors who had come by the day this happened, who had wanted me to go visit with his wife but my mate said I was busy, told me he knew that my mate was going to try and kill me. The look my mate had, my neighbor had seen before and that's why he tried to get me to come over and stay with his wife.

My God had been with me and kept me safe. Thank you, Jesus!

I stayed on the mountain till the morning. My mate was to be sent home the night after I packed a couple suitcases and got ready to leave at that daybreak. I stayed up on the mountain as it was cold and we had a cat so I had to keep the wood heater burning so the pipes and the cat wouldn't freeze.

My mate had shot my dog the same night all this happened about ten minutes before he came in to get me. He threw my coat at me. I had heard a shot and when he came in his boots had blood on them. I asked what the shot was about and he told me he killed my dog. I now knew it was because my dog would have attacked him when he saw I was being hurt.

On the 5th of December, I came off the mountain and stayed at a lady friend's house. The next morning December 6, I was on a bus for home, where my mother lives.

I sold my vehicle to come here as I wasn't in any shape to drive. When I got home, friends met me at the bus depot and I stayed with them for one night. The next day the Salvation Army got me a motel room. I sure thank God for the Salvation Army! After one night in the motel the Safe House phoned to let me know they now had a bed for me.

While I was there I got in touch with the head of the Care Giver's and let them know who I was and who my mother was. They were happy that one of the family members was now living in town as my mother had been living in a very bad hotel with a man who was a very heavy gambler. The Care Giver's couldn't get in the room most of the time and they were all very worried about my mom.

I phoned my mom on Christmas Eve and right away she said to me, "You are in town." When I asked her how she knew, she said, "Just this morning I looked up to the ceiling of my room and there I saw you, in the corner with a light all around you." She said, "I knew you had come to save me."

After I found an apartment for myself, I went and visited mom and her friend.

Mom was so thin and I knew something was wrong with her mind also. I talked her friend into letting me take her to the doctor. He said sure as he was confident that the doctor wouldn't do anything as mom hadn't seen him in at least two years. She had only been going to the lab once a month to get her blood checked.

You see mom's friend wanted to keep mom with him because after the rent was paid, her check and his went for gambling. At the time I saw them both it was a couple days after they had gotten paid and all that was in their fridge was ½ cup of milk and a bottle of wine. Mom did not drink alcohol. I went to the store and got them some food but didn't leave them any money.

Meanwhile, I had also phoned mom's doctor and told him I suspectedmom had dementia, so he set up an appointment right away. My beautiful mother didn't even have boots and hershoes had holes in them as we walkedin the snow.

The doctor took one look at her and told me, "You can't handle this" and made an appointment with a psychiatrist. The appointment was week away. We went back to the hotel and I told her friend that the doctor wanted to do some testson mom. I would have to bring her backnext week. He agreed.

I had been phoning mom every day, when I was on the mountain, begging her to move in with friends until I could come home to her.

There was a woman who ran the switchboard there that often told me to mind my own business and leave my mother do what ever she wanted. I believe she was listening to our phone calls. As the hotel they were living in was also the gambling location, the hotel was making a lot of money from their pay checks. Their pay checks wentto the gambling machines and this switchboard person who worked the desk didn't want to see mom move.

A week after mom's family doctor's appointment I got mom to see the psychiatrist and right away he said she was in the early of middle stages of dementia. He then got her booked for an evaluation one week later which was the 13th of January.

When we got back to the hotel, I told mom's friend the truth that mom had dementia and had to go into the hospital on the 13th. The next day I received a phone call from a police officer telling me I could not go on the property where the hotel was and I could not be in touch with my mother. Her friend and the desk clerk said I was harassing my own mother.

The police officer also told me that mom didn't have to go to the hospital unless she wanted to. I asked him to come and talk with me in person, not just on the phone. He said that wasn't necessary.

I was very worried as I didn't know what to do so I prayed. I realized that the police man had heard one side of the story from an 89 year old woman, with dementia, and an 85 year old man who was telling her what to say. LaterI found out that mom was afraid she would be locked up and never get to see him again.

The desk clerk, I believe, also told the police I was just trying to break mom and her friend up. She actually ended up losing her job after quite a commotion. The Caregiver and I could not get momto go to the hospital. The head doctor had the police and ambulance go to the hotel and bring mom to the hospital.

The doctor there said mom was dying from mal-nutrition and said she wouldn't have lived more than a week longer if she had not been hospitalized. God's timing is always perfect. Mom stayed in the hospital over three months before we could find her a good nursing home.

While she was there I took sick and was rushed to the hospital. I had no potassium, what so ever and my heart, blood pressure and I guess every thing else was shutting down. The doctors didn't think I would make it.

God is good! Both mom and I were in the hospital at the same time while the nurses would bring mom down to see me.

Well it's been two and half years since then and mom is 91 years old. In October she will be 92 years young. Every night on the phone we say the Lord's Prayer together and she doesn't missa beat. Her friend died last year from lung cancer but, Praise God, he started praying and believing before he passed on. God is good and so merciful!

My mom still always knows who I am and we are so blessed to have this time together. I believe we all have miracles happening to us. Life itself is a miracle.

I sat with mom's friend in his last days and I praise God so much as I felt no anger or desire to put blame on him. I thank God for allowing me to have had these experiences.

Anonymous Believer

Miracle 7

Three Years Remission

I have had many experiences of miracles large and small. This one occurred with the knowledge and concurrence of a physician.

Some years ago I developed Glaucomain both eyes, which developed into cataracts. My eye specialist arranged for me to go to a clinic in Calgary which would have charged an extra $300.00.

Ten days before the operation, a prayer leader called "Julio" from Columbia visited here in Medicine Hat. I attended his meeting and he did not say I would be cured, but that I would see clearer. After prayer at the meeting, when I got home, I did see clearer.

I reported my eye sight ability to my doctor and he said I did not need the operation. I had a remission for three years and eventually had the right cataract replaced with a plexi-glass, free. The other eye had too little sight to operate on.

Thank you, Jesus, for the ability to see to write this miracle story, by myself.

John H.

Retired Teacher

Miracle 8

Two Pairs of Shoes

In the mid 1980's, I had become a single parent with three young children and had a whole of $25.00 to my name one day and needed two pairs of shoes. I prayed all the way to the store that I would have enough money to buy two pairs of shoes and be able to drive 35 miles home again. I got to the mall in Medicine Hat and they happened to have a sale on and I was able to buy the shoes and have just enough money left over to get home again.

It may seem like a small miracle but at the time it was a big one for me, since I always tithed what little I had. God always came through for me at times when it was the most difficult.

Also, around that same time, I received a night full of what seemed to be a slide show of heaven. I saw Mary, holding the baby Jesus. She would sit up and then lie down and then she would be gone. I saw St. Joseph also and St. Teresa of the Child Jesus and many other saints, as well as my grandmother and some other people I did not recognize. Many of the saints were dressed in white gowns.

After I saw all of this I was able to write down some of the names. I kept the little book with those names. It was given to me, I believe, in order that my faith in God would grow. It has and ever since then, I have found it much easierto believe.

I have received many more miracles over the years but these two stood outfor me at this time.

God bless you and yours.

Ria W.

Bookkeeper

Miracle 9

Miracle of Flight #1549 was that of Divine Mercy

We've had a 'Miracle on 34th Street' and now we have a "Miracle on the Hudson," said New York Gov. David Paterson. Fred Berretta, one of the passengers on that US Air Flight # 1549, who was interviewed that very evening on national television, said that it was definitely a "miracle".

The city of New York surveillance video footage of the US Airways jet forced to make an emergency landing in the Hudson River, after both its engines failed, clearly showed God's incredible Divine Mercy at work. It was as if God was supporting it with His huge merciful hands.

In his first public comments about what it was like to safely land a passenger jet in the Hudson River, US Airways pilot Chesley "Sully"

Sullenberger, who was at the controls of the Airbus 320 aircraft, described the ordeal as "surreal".

In a brief interview with ESPN the night before the Super Bowl—where he and the crew were given a standing ovation –Sullenberger said that while he was guiding the plane to a splash landing he felt "calm on the outside, turmoil on the inside."

These terms "miracle", "surreal", and "calm" uttered by the crew, the passengers and the onlookers all detail exactly an act of God. But why would God show us His miraculous hands at work in supporting that plane, calming the crew, and arranging such a perfect rescue?

Why does God perform miracles anyway? He performs miracles to witness to His presence. Is there really a good reason why God miraculously set this plane down so gently and saved all of the crew and passengers? Why at this time and for what reason? It must be to bring attention to, and reveal, His Divine Mercy.

Fred Berretta, the passenger that was sitting over the left engine, who was interviewed on national TV by Lou Dobbs, Wolf Blitzer and Bill O'Reilly, has come forward with more details of the miraculous safe landing of Flight #1549. He has a remarkable story about his prayer just before that incredible crash.

Fred, a pilot himself, did tell Bill O'Reilly that he was "convinced that it was a miracle" and that he was "still trying to process the whole thing". But just nine days after the crash, Fred sent an e-mail to Vinny Flynn, the world famous Divine Mercy author witnessing to him the astonishing details of the last minutes of the flight and what led up to it!

He explained to Vinny that he had just purchased his book "Seven Secretsof the Eucharist" and had read it, up until just after take-off. He said "he had just closed his eyes to reflect on the incredible insights your book gave me regarding the Eucharist". Vinny is a renowned expert on Divine Mercy and has included in the book some of the incredible words of Jesus about the Eucharist. Saint Faustina had recorded these words of Jesus in her diary called "Divine Mercy in My Soul".

Before we go on with the rest of the story, it must be explained that Jesus revealed many more things, over a seven year period, to St. Faustina, that she recorded in her diary. One of the most important things that Jesus told her was about praying during the hour that He died. It is well known that Jesus died at about 3p.m. Jesus told her, "In this hour, I will refuse nothing to the soul that makes a request of Me in virtue of My Passion." (taken from the Diary of Saint Faustina, entry#1320.)

It was right smack in the middle of this "Hour of Great Mercy", at about 3:30 p.m., when the plane was going down, that Fred remembered this incredible promise of Our Lord Jesus and made a request. He testified to

Vinny Flynn "I thought about the words Jesus said (about that special promise), that nothing would be refused if asked for during the "Hour of Mercy". I really thought there was a good chance myself and others would die that day, but I asked God to be merciful to us."

Fred went on to tell Vinny "I just want you to know that your book gave me comfort as we were going down, and for that I am grateful. I know a lot of people prayed on that plane, and I believe the Miracle on the Hudson was a testament to the mercy of God, and a sign of hope." It was during this hour that our Lord Jesus' heart was pierced by a lance on the Cross and His blood and water gushed forth as a fountain of mercy for the whole world.

Fred Berretta will be giving his witness for the first time in public at the Divine Mercy Conference in Orlando, on Saturday, February 21ˢᵗ at the Queen of the Universe Shrine. Vinny Flynn, the author of the "Seven Secrets of The Eucharist" will be one of the main speakers along with Fr. Gramlich from the Divine Mercy Shrine in Stockbridge. Vinny's book on the Seven Secrets of the Eucharist will be available at the conference. And just maybe, Fred and Vinny will autograph one for you!

Anonymous

Miracle 10

The Throne at the End of My Bed

This is my special bedtime miracle the night before my operation with in the Medicine Hat Hospital.

I have been a believing, praying Christian since a very young girl and later in my life I experienced the presence of the Holy Trinity.

I was in my retired time of life and I came due to have a serious operation. As always, before retiring for the night, I prayed to God, to steady and guide the surgeon's hands the next day while they operated on me. I prayed that Jesus, My Heavenly Father and the Holy Spirit would be with me as I went through the operation and also after wards while recovering.

After I had been praying awhile, while sitting on my bed in the dark, I, for some unknown reason, glanced upwards, towards the foot of my bed. There I was, wide awake, sitting in the darkened bedroom, only to be enlightened with a beautiful "Holy Trinity" vision.

There before me was a Throne that went to the ceiling. Centered in the middle of the Throne was a mist with, behind the foggy essence, three figure heads composed in a triangle. Behind the towering Throne were four huge, brilliant, white angels with tremendously long extended wings that reached from the ceiling down around the bottom of the Throne.

In amazement and awe, I knew instantly that my Precious Jesus with His Father and His Precious Holy Spirit had heard my prayers and was confirming their precious presence.

Moments later the vision dispersed and I was momentarily excited and numbed all in the same outcome. I sat there in total amazement, my senses tingling and a bit in shock. I tried to lie down to go to sleep but was so thrilled and touched by this Glorious encounter that I had to get up, out of bed, go to the kitchen and digest in total silence God's magnificent interaction with me.

The next day by the Grace of God, my operation went perfectly and yes, I thank Him eternally!

Erma

Miracle 11

Midnight Conversation

My husband and I were fast asleep. I was lying beside my husband, facing away from him. He also was faced away from me.

All of a sudden my husband turned around quickly to face my back and knocked on my back like a "door knock." He said in his half sleep "Knock, knock, there is someone that is at the door for you.

I quickly turned around awake wondering what my husband was doing. Cory turned back into his sleeping position, facing the other way. I said out loud, "What are you doing?" Cory briefly commented back to me, "I am dreaming." I too then resorted back to my original sleeping position.

On closing my eyes, I tried to resume sleep, when I heard a soft message, directed to me as a question. "Do you want me to take Satan from you?" Immediately I listened and in my spiritI responded, "Yes, Jesus I do!" Jesus responded, "Through your book, I will."

Within seconds of our conversation I was alone again. Praise Jesus, God our Holy Father and The Precious Holy Spirit! I believe this spiritual conversation was a prelude to something wonderful coming into my life. I am not sure what blessing to look forward to, but I know God does.

After the conversation I pulled the bed covers close and tried to resume sleep, but my body could not rest. The Holy Spirit seemed very strong to me asI felt it was very vital that I record what had just happened.

First of all, Jesus knocked on my husband's heart's door to reach throughto me. To me that say's that my precious husband, Cory and I are one, not only,in marriage, but also in heart. Second ofall, Jesus has something very wonderful to inject into our lives and He wanted to tell me.

Thank you wonderful Savior, for like Your Holy Word says, You do walk and talk with us, if we only listen.

February 9, I sat down at 1:00 a.m. to record this very special encounter with my Jesus because Jesus said to.

L. K.

Child of God

Miracle 12

Fr. Gino C. Violini: The DayIt Rained At Cowley

Cowley is a small town nestled in the foothills of the Rockies in southern Alberta. Its little wooden church ofSt. Joseph's stood forlorn and poorly attended for many a season.

This situation was soon brightenedby the cheerful presence of Father Gino C. Violini who was transferred there from Schuler on July 18, 1946.

Schuler was a job well done, during the last two years of his pastor-ship no fallen away Catholics were to be found within the boundaries of his parish. Father had learned German and used it freely in the pastoral care of his flock.

Bishop Francis P. Carroll decided that the parish of St. Joseph"s, Cowley, needed Father Gino"s spiritual energy and faith-filled optimism.

On arriving at Cowley, Father Violini was met by a group of people who told him that Cowley did not need a priest, and that whenever the need arose, the bishop would be duly informed. They also said that they did not want to see Father Gino reading his breviary in public, or going about wearing his cassock.

A total of nine were present for Mass that first Sunday. Father delivered his best sermon that morning. Yet only four faithful returned for Mass the following week. Even two years of zeal, hard work and sacrifice did not seem to put a dent in the indifferent spirit of his parish. Or did it?

There were, for example, weeks when he had to get by on bread and dandelions. There were winter mornings when he awoke to find snow on the floor and on his bedding where it had filtered through the walls of his old rectory. There were mission stations where the water in the cruets was frozen solid by offertory time. That first Christmas his collection from all sources amounted to a dollar and thirteen cents.

Of spiritual and material poverty, Father Gino had his fill.

But there was one bright spot. A group of generous souls in Cowley could not do enough for their parish priest as soon as they heard of his dire conditions. Had it no been for their outstanding generosity, Father Gino might, indeed, have starved. Among this group there were the Lamires, the Blais, the Diamonds and many others.

Outside of this circle however, Father Gino looked upon Cowley as a write off, and he wanted out as soon as possible.

With this in mind he wrote numerous letters, one sixteen pages in length, begging the bishop for a move.

The bishop, however, rejected all of Father Gino's reasons for wanting a transfer, and told him to stay put at Cowley. He had full confidence in

Father's ability to bring about a Catholic revival in this long neglected parish.

This was a great let down. But an even greater shock was already in the works.

It happened on the feast of Corpus Christi, 1948, which fell on June 5th that year, the tenth anniversary of Father Violini's ordination to the priesthood.

He arose early that morning as was his habit and went directly to the church. There he found the front door hanging by one hinge and the windows all smashed in. This was the beginningof a series of events that would end in the most spectacular happening of Father Gino's priesthood.

Inside the church, he could see that nothing had been spared. The walls and statues were in shambles. But his greatest fear of all was for the tabernacle.

He did not have to look far. He found part of it near the door. Being made of wood, it had been smashed to pieces. And there he saw, scattered down the main aisle of the church, the consecrated Host from the tabernacle.

One by one he picked up the Hosts, counting them as he went along. He recovered them all, but the large Benediction Host was missing.

Immediately, he alerted Father Michael Harrington of the Crowsnest deanery. Father Harrington, with the go-ahead from Bishop Carroll, initiated a massive search for the Blessed Sacrament.

From the neighboring towns of Bellevue, Hillcrest, Blairemore, Coleman, and from as far away a Michel and Natal in British Columbia a search party numbering about fifteen hundred persons was assembled. Yet Father Gino's appeal in his own parish turned up no willing hands.

All that day under heavy rains the big search party combed long stretches of the wide grassy area on each side of highway #3.

In the meantime two suspects were picked up at Cowley by the R.C.M.P., and were being questioned at Blairemore. A pick up truck which they had stolen and abandoned was found, but at this point nothing was seen of the Blessed Sacrament.

After prolonged questioning by the R.C.M.P., Father Violini got permission to speak to the two suspects. He recognized them immediately as the two young men who sat by him and chatted with him during a baseball game the day before.

They had told Father that they came from Lethbridge and were in the Pass looking for work in the mines. In the police station Father Gino chatted with them in his usual friendly manner. He explained to them the meaning of the Blessed Sacrament and how much it means to Catholics. Then, in one sweeping act of kindness, he offered to drop all charges against them in return for their help in finding the missing Host.

"How much reparation", he reasoned, "would be done by putting these boysbehind bars for fourteen to twenty years?"

The men were touched by Father Gino's explanation of the Blessed Sacrament, and were truly remorseful for what had happened. One finally admitted to breaking into the church and stealing a round, white object, which he discarded later through the window of the police car as he was being taken into custody. He did not know what it was, but fearedit might be used as evidence against him if found on his person.

Both suspects described in detail the part of the highway where they abandoned the Blessed Sacrament. They expressed sorrow for the trouble they caused, and offered to go out there, handcuffed and under police guard, to show Father Violini the exact spot.

Father was of the opinion that if the Blessed Sacrament was as the two men had said: lying on the grass of the highway shoulder, it would surely have been found by one of the search parties, or else dissolved by the heavy rains. Nevertheless, he and Sergeant Parsons of the Pincher Creek R.C.M.P. drove back along the highway to the place indicated by the suspects.

It was now approaching six o'clock in the evening. The day's rain was over and the sky was starting to clear. As they rounded a bend in the road east of Bellevue they were astounded to see the Host suspended in the air beside the highway and displaying beautiful rays of colored light.

Before the police car had come to a complete halt, Father Gino had the door opened and was rushing toward this amazing sight. The police sergeant came running close behind.

As Father reached the spot, (it was the exact place described by the two suspects) he knelt in adoration, overwhelmed by the wonder before his eyes and the joy that filled his soul. The sergeant, a non-Catholic, did the same, landing in a pool of mud left by the rains.

Getting to his feet, Father reached toward the suspended Host and took it gently in his hands. It looked as white and as fresh as the day he consecratedit. At this point he heard these gentle words: "Father Gino, please take me back to Cowley."

It was a moment in his life he says he will never forget. To this day he weepsin recounting the extraordinary event, the meaning of which always remains clear and overpowering to him. Here was Jesus on the road asking to be brought back to a desecrated church and to a parish from which Father Ginohad long wanted to be free.

On the way back to Cowley, Sergeant Parson's eyes constantly left the road to look at Father Gino's hands and the wonder he held there.

The events surrounding the church break-in and finding of the Blessed Sacrament were thoroughly examined by the bishop and his authorities who arrived in Cowley on the following day.

Father Michael Harrington, who later became bishop of Kamloops, British Columbia, got permission to consume the miraculous Host, a privilege keenly missed by Father Gino, The bishop, however, granted Father Violini the special privilege of rededicating the church of St. Joseph's. Having prayed for some time amid the devastated interior, the bishop turned to Father Gino and said prophetically: "great changes for the better will soon take place in this parish".

Soon after, Sergeant Parsons, who had seen the Host suspended in the air, asked Father Violini for instructions in the Catholic Faith. He was joined by his wife and children, and later by his two constables from Pincher Creek. All were baptized into the Faith by Father Gino. This was only the beginning of many graces that would be showered on the people of Cowley.

As time went on, more and more inactive Catholics returned to the sacramental life of the Church. The parish mission became a celebrated event in the town. As the mission hour approached, the beer hall shut down and the patrons, of whom a large portion were non-Catholic, filed out carrying bar stools, to sit in and hear the fiery sermons at St. Joseph's. Even the pot-belly stove had to be removed from the church to make room for everyone.

The little wooden church, which not long ago housed a mere handful of worshippers, was now full to overflowing each Sunday. Truly, God was blessing this parish as the bishop had foretold.So much so, that the next problem was where to fit so many parishioners.

But God had other than architectural designs in mind for Father Gino. On February 3, f1951 he was transferred to Gleichen, a town near the Blackfoot Indian Reserve, sixty-five miles east of Calgary.

The news of Father Gino's transfer came as a shock to the people of St. Joseph's parish. Many hearts were sad. Some were bitter. A few were determinedto block the move. Yet, much as Father

Gino loved his Cowley people, and dreaded the thought of leaving them, the voice of the bishop was the voice of Jesus Christ. And the sweet memory of that voice by the highway near Bellevue, "Father Gino, please take me back to Cowley" had taught him much.

The number of well-wishers who turned out to bid the Catholic priest of Cowley a fond farewell cut through all religious line. The non-Catholic ministers of the Russian Doukhobor sect gave resounding speeches praising Father Violini for holding out a helping hand to them in their time of need, and for breaking the long bitter prejudice of the people against them. It was an event that stirred everyone's heart, and a joyful demonstration that any resentment that might have existed before against a resident priest was indeed past history.

In the early hours of February 3, before anyone was stirring, Father Gino Violini drove away from the mountains and people he had come to love so much, and whose spiritual welfare he held so dear.

The emotions of the people could be summed up in the words of an old man who sat forlornly on the steps of St. Joseph's church, lamenting: "O my poor soul! What am I going to do now, that Father is gone?"

Rev. Fr. G.C. Violini

Father Gino Cresens Violini was born July 28, 1907 at Urbino, Italy. Baptized and confirmed at birth, third son of Giovanni (John) and Louise Violini. He arrived in Canada May 4, 1910 and first settled at Bankhead, near Banff. Family moved to Calgary 1911. Attended Sunnyside Bungalow Public Elementary in 1913 until classes opened for Catholic children in Sunnyside in 1914. Attended Sunnyside Bungalow Public Elementary in 1913 until classes opened for Catholic children in Sunnyside in 1914.Two years later St. John's School was officially opened. He completed his high school at St. Mary's Boy's School and entered St. Joseph's Seminary,

Edmonton September 1929. AttendedSt. Peter's London, Ontario (1932) where he studied Theology. He took sick 1934 and returned to Calgary to recuperate. He then returned to Seminary September 1936 and was ordained by Bishop Francis P. Carroll, June 5, 1938 at St. Mary's Cathedral, Calgary. He was first appointed to St. Anne's church on June 20th, 1938 and his second appointmentto St. Patrick's Church, Medicine Hat in October of 1938. Next he was appointedto Schuler, July 18 of 1940. He then was appointed to Cowley, July 18th of 1946. Following that he was appointed to Gleichen February, 1951. And lastlywas appointed to St. Mary's Cathedral September 20, 1962 and retired from Cathedral April of1980.

He celebrated Golden Jubilee of Ordination June 5, 1988, during the Marian Year (1987-88), and the 75th year anniversary of the Diocese of Calgary. Deo Gratias.

Wilbert Zinger

Miracle 13

Miracle on #3 Highway

What a Difference a Day Makes

It was back in March 26th, of 2000, on a Sunday, a beautiful afternoon. The type of day that beckons you to come out and test what Nature has to offer. Wear a coat or not to wear a coat. It was that kind of day. I decided to shovel all the gravel from the back of the old '79 GMC. It is gravel we need to spread on the ramp that leads out of the Dairy Queen drive thru in Downtown Medicine Hat. An, Alberta, City, also known for its very hot summers and extremely cold winters.

At about 3 o'clock I took off to our acreage, four miles south of the city. A short drive and it would only take a few minutes to unload the gravel on that road I was building. Mission completed and back to the D.Q. for a cup of coffee with friends. "Doug you look tired you should go home and lay down" they said. I was tired but not hurting. I took their advice and started home with the lemons my wife asked me to bring home to sprinkle on the salmon that was being cooked for supper.

On my way home a sharp pain came across my chest and I knew I was in trouble. My home is near the hospital so I decided to go for the hospital. The problem is I became disoriented and ended up on the highway going to Lethbridge. Gasping for breath I slammed on the brakes and stopped in the middle of the highway, opened the door of the truck, but the seatbelt held me back. "Who's that drunk?" a driver yelled. "Learn to drive you idiot", complained a motorist as he gave me the finger.

Finally a gentleman wearing a baseball cap, driving a car loaded with young people, did stop and along with another motorist managed to pull that limp, 265 pound body on to the ground. The man with the cap applied C.P.R. while the other ran for help. A lady passing by had a cell phone and phoned 911 and an ambulance appeared from out of nowhere. This fellow doesn't look healthy one of the paramedics explained with a look of sadness chiseled into his face. He looks familiar whispered another EMT. Your right it's Mr. Burgess, you know Dough Burgess from the Dairy Queen. "Oh God he looks just like my Dad" said the fellow who ran for help. A policeman bent down looked over the situation and called for help. "Need more back up on the #3 highway in front of the Esso Service".

After what seamed like hours they loaded me into the ambulance for the trip to the hospital, a trip that reminded me of the song: "What a difference a day makes".

I have been told that more deaths occur during the weekend than during the week. It was just my luck, me arriving, on a Sunday.

The doctors started working on me as soon as the paramedics rolled into emergency. With a tube down the neck, needles in the arms, oxygen in the face and paddles on the chest, they decided to phone his family because it doesn't look like he will make it. The room was full of doctors and nurses, policemen and firemen and of coarse the paramedics. A policeman called dispatch and had the police contact my wife, "don't tell her how bad he is. Send a car around". Send a car to the "Q" for the son and daughter, they are always there.

With the family waiting out in the hallway the people in green moved around the table like a well oiled machine. Then the box with the graph stopped going up and down, started to level off and then stopped. The room exploded, the medical staff crawled around me pushing, poking and slapping but to no avail. Mr. Burgess the ice cream man, the man who devoted 36 years of his life to serving the best milkshakes and sundaes the town has ever enjoyed, was dead.

Dr. Wagle the heart doctor was writing down the time 4:14 time of death. Nurse Combs was in the side office making out the tow tag. "Does his name end with two S's"?

The room was silent. "O God, please help" a voice from the back cut thru the sterile air. Nurse Combs is a very religious person, she believes, and so did everyone who was in that room that day. Let me explain. Nurse Combs asked everyone to hold hands and pray. They did, a silent prayer. Not long, just enough for the tears to fall upon my body, like tear drops from Angels above.

Let's clean up the room ordered Dr. Wagle, his voice crackling, his eyes red. Twenty minutes had gone by since that black box stopped bouncing up and down. Now it was time to move on. What happened next is what miracles are made of. As the nurse was pulling the sheet over my remains, a very faint breath came flowing from my mouth.

He is alive, he is alive! Yes, he is alive! Don't leave the room, Mr. Burgess is alive! In disbelief it was back to action full speed. "If he lives the night we will fly him to Calgary", Dr. Wagle explained in a hurried voice.

I went to the Foothills Hospital the next day.

I always liked Calgary. There is always a lot to do., fantastic shopping, plenty of car lots to cruise and a wonderful selection of classic restaurants with also very up to date hotels. But this is not a pleasure trip....it is a life or death trip.

I finally woke up three days later in the ICU in Calgary. I don't remember leaving or arriving. There is a lot I don't remember in Medicine Hat, just three days ago. I do remember thinking out loud.....

"What a Difference a Day Makes"

It was very early in the morning when my eyes started to stretch, a blink here and a blink there. Out of the mist should appear, Lil, Bob and Denise: my family. Soon after, over in the corner standing, I saw Jim my brother, my mentor, and his wife. Jim and Hazel Penney had come all the way from Lethbridge, Alberta.

The days and months that followed consisted of a full slate of tests. The eco gram, the mag-a-gram, blood tests morning and night, stress tests, an-a-plastic, oxygen tests, ex-rays, check for cholesterol, the kidneys test and on it went.

Finally after loosing 65 pounds and spending 68 days in the hospital I was told I could go home.

I asked, "Doctor how long will I live?" The doctor said, "I would estimate 3 years".

It's hard to believe, but I think I am going to miss this place. Rosie the house cleaner always had incorrigible stories to tell and loved to collect lapel pins. Nurse Carol, who was going to have laser done on one of her eyes was very nervous. The doctors were tops as most would ask how the "Miracle Man" was doing? Dr. Peter Genogra called me Lazarus.

Dr. Genogra asked if I would mind letting a few University Students interview me. These were the people on their way to becoming full fledge Doctors. Sure bring them in. Seven walked into the room formed a circle around my bed and pulled the curtain. A Chinese gentleman looking over a clipboard was the first to speak. "Mr. Burgess is it true you died?" Without hesitation I answered "yes". A nice looking dark haired lady asked if I saw a hand or did smoke appear. I thought for a few seconds and replied, "No but out of the corner of my eye I saw this bright light. It started to move closer and closer and twisted and turned, bigger and bigger. It stopped. It was a chocolate covered cherry blizzard from the Dairy Queen". They pulled the curtain and left.

Two days later I left for home, 65 pounds lighter and with 20% of my heart. My son Bob drove up from the Hat in the new Denali we purchased just months before my heart attack. All the way back I kept humming that tune......

"What a difference a day makes".

We made it home and it was great to be with my wife, Lil and all of my family and friends again. It's the home we bought back in 1968 and just recently added a large sunroom, a room that was going to be my recoup center for the next few weeks. I had to know thetruth, I needed the facts.

Who were the people who pulled me out of the truck? Who made that important phone call to 911? How long was I lying in silence at the hospital?

Well my son told me, "Well Dad, you know that fellow that gave you C.P.R. that we have been telling you about"? "Yes", I answered. He is a cancer Doctor from Lethbridge and we have been sending him flowers and up dates on you everyday. And the other man is Bruce Barton's boy. He has been coming to our store since he was a baby. The ladyon the cell phone was Mrs. Thompson, you know the Insurance Family?"

Boy, what a small world. I know all these people, except the Doctor from Lethbridge. All those people that signed that giant "get well card". Yes, I am a lucky man!

I remember reading the Calgary Sun after I started to feel human again. Some of the stories brought tears to my eyes. One story was about a 21 year old Stampede Queen Contestant who fell off her horse and died. Another was about a 21 year old, blown off the back of a truck while trying to hold a 4 x 8 sheet of plywood down. I remember telling Dr. Mitchell about these stories in the paper and wondering why them and not me? As he was working the wire through my veins he said "Don't waste your time trying to answer that question, just concentrate on the time you have left on this earth". You know that was very good advice, because I would never have learned the answer.

One of my best friends carves brick walls. Jim Marshall carves wall all over the world. Jim carved one for the Hospital in Lethbridge, Alberta. I told him that I have to go to Lethbridge to present a gift to the doctor who placed oxygen in my brain so that I could function and not be a vegetable. He asked me what I had as a gift. I told him that I checked with my family and my daughter, who is an EMT, reminded me not to give money because if something would happen to you we could sue the doctor...no... after what he did for me, fat chance. So Jim and I made a phone call to the Canadian Mint and told them what happened. They suggested a gold watch in the shape of a 50 cent piece, with on it reading, "Miracles still happen. Thanks for beinga part of one March 26th, 2000". After the watch arrived at my home, I wrapped it and made a little thank you note. The next day Jim Marshall and I drove to Lethbridge, with me to deliver the watch and the message to the man who was responsible of breathing life back into my body. Jim was going to take picturesof the brick wall that he had carved and installed at the hospital.

Outside of the City by a few miles I made a call to Dr. Hollands office on my cell. "Hello. I would like to talk to the doctor who saved my life." "Who isthis?" "My name is Doug Burgess and Dr. Holland saved me in Medicine Hat". "Oh yes....we know you. You're the "Highway

Man" .... Dr. Holland would love to see you again...where are you?" "Just out side of your office, by 10 minutes." The nurse said, "Please drive up to the front door and walk right in. We will be waiting for you".

In my life time I have had a lot on nice experiences. The people of Medicine Hat have been really nice and have treated me with love and respect but please believe me what happened that afternoon will always be etched in my mind.

When Jim and I opened the door of the clinic and moved toward the waiting room, everyone in the waiting room stood up and clapped as we walked in. The nurses came out of the various offices and then the doctors. Finally there was complete silence, and in slow motion a door opened and out stepped the doctor I came to see. We both froze in our steps. Looking and crying like long lost brothers. We approached each other and hugged. Then Dr. Holland said, "The hair on my neck is standing straight up. I never though I would ever see you alive again".

I explained that I had brought a gift, a Thank You Gift for helping me out on Highway #3 that Sunday afternoon.

He opened the package and afterward said to me and to all the patients, nurses and other doctors in the waiting room. "Your not going to believe this but I said to my wife this morning....I have to get a new watch, mine is broken"!

"What a Difference a Day Makes"!

Miracle Relived by

Mr. Douglas Cletion Burgess

Of Medicine Hat, Alberta, Canada

I am retired at 63, with 80% of my heart gone.

I have learned that no matter how young you feel or how strong you think you are, STOP and think about your HEART. Your heart is pushing you day and night, everyday and every night!

Miracle 14

Montana Highway Miracle

On the way to Bonneville, Salt Flats, Utah, we were travelling in our 1940 Ford when between Butte, Montana and Dillon, Montana, the oil line of our car broke and we lost all of our oil in our car. We pulled to shoulder of the highway and found out we didn't have any extra oil in the truck. Harvey was going to thumb a ride to Dillon for oil.

A few motorists passed by us when then we noticed a newer motor-home coming towards us. As it approached us, they turned into the lane opposite us. We were on the right shoulder and they were now driving in the left lane.

It seemed they were planning to pass us by in the far lane.

Within seconds after them passing us, they took an immediate pullover to the right hand shoulder and stopped! Harvey and I presumed they stopped to help us. Harvey immediately got out and went to the driver's side window, of the Motor-home, which was opened just a crack. Harvey proceeded to ask the stranger in motor-home if they had any extra oil to sell us. The driver then passed the key through the cracked window and said, "Go back in the storage box and take as much oil as you need".

When Harvey got the oil, he went back to the driver, gave back the keys and asked him, "How much do we owe you"?

The driver was pleasant and said, "Have a good trip. Don't worry about the oil." He then put the motor-home in gear and left.

After fixing our car we headed for Dillon, Montana. The first service station we came to we stopped to get more oil, when we noticed the familiar motor-home that helped us, filling gas.

Right away, Harvey bought four quarts of oil to give back to the man in the motor-home. We went to the side door of the motor-home, knocked and there we were greeted by the drivers wife. We thanked her for stopping to help us and gave her the 4 quarts of oil we had borrowed earlier.

Amazingly enough she proceeded to tell us that they had no intentions to stop for us. However, as they drovealong side of us, their motor-home diedor quit. They had no choice but to pullover right in front of us. The amazing part was that after we got oil from them, the man turned over the key and the motor-home started again and drove away.

For some reason, they were literally put in our path to help us and we thank them from the bottom of our hearts. Again, God knows when we need help and now we would like to say "Thank-you".

Anne and Harvey

The 40ies and 50ies,
Car Club Members

Miracle 15

A Spiritual Walk with God

Thank you, for this opportunity to share with you about God's hand on my life. I grew up on my parent's farm about eight miles west of Richmound, Saskatchewan.

At the age of twelve I was helping with the harvest when I backed into the power takeoff providing power to the combine and immediately my pants were caught pulling me down. Dad reached out and pulled me to safety leaving me without any pants on and only slightly bruised.

Only a few years later at the age of sixteen I was on the tractor with my sister when I fell off the tractor to the ground and had the tiller run over me. I got up from the ground and walked away unhurt.

Years later in 1968, I was driving home to Richmound when applying the brakes caused me to lose control of the car on the gravel road causing it to roll. There were two other people in the car with me. I was hurt and another individual ended up paralyzed while the third escaped unhurt.

Because it was a single vehicle accident there were charges and I was to go to trial. The authorities proceeded to examine the car for mechanical problems and found out the car had previous problems so when I applied the brakes, the right front wheel locked up making me lose control.

Concerned over the upcoming court appearance I wrote a note to God and buried it. I released it to God, though I didn't fully understand it at all, how, but God worked it out so I did not have to go to court.

Years later, a man named Dennis, began working at Wittke's (1997) in First stage, where I worked. We began talking about God. Dennis was always available to answer questions about God and so we talked numerous times. One result was, I got asked by Bill Caceres to attend a bible study. I decided to go. I have been attending Ted Herman's study ever since.

Then on September 19 of 2000, the study group got me a bible and I began to read it regularly. Soon after that, God woke me up one night and told me that my name is in "God's book of Life".

July of 2002, Dennis and I went to the Miracle Channel Grand opening and dedication of their new building. What a blessed time we had! We were in meetings from 9:30 a.m. to 10:30 p.m. During the morning service God spoke to me and shared that the Miracle Channel is the store house for the Nation of Canada. Later in the afternoon we went to the ribbon cutting ceremony, when again God spoke and shared that He is going to touch the hearts of people like never before.

I thank God for what He has done in my life and for those He has brought across my path that have helped me with my walk with Him.

Here are some Miracle stories on my journey since 2000.

December 7, 2004

I had steel tubing with a flat bar on top of the saw horses. The flat bar and steel tubing were oily and wet from the snow. As I lifted my end of the flat bar, the opposite end fell off and there as I was standing as the opposite end flew over my head. I realized I could have been badly hurt. The first thing I could think of was to Thank God for saving me.

September 2, 2005

It was Friday and before I went homeI took the fuse out of the saw for safety reasons. On the Monday morning backat work about 7:30 a.m., I went to cutsome pipe on the saw. I started up the saw and cut it half way through the pipe when all of a sudden it stopped. I checked the fuse and realized the fuse was still out from Friday. This had to be a miracle that the saw worked with out the fuse in the saw. The Holy Spirit spoke to me and said, "The power I put in the saw, I will put also the same power in you."

October 21, 2006

Ken and Ron did a spiritual workshop at Holy Family Parish. The first Vision I received was a building with many rooms with doors in it. The first room had many cob webs. Then the room got very bright and all the cob webs were gone. I believe this vision was stating to me the "Lord's Glory".

The second room had a circle of fire in the middle of the room. I believe it was the "Cleansing of my sins".

The third room was half filled with green grass and the other half was a field filled with the ripe harvest of wheat. The fourth room showed my ring that I got from work. The ring was so bright that it shone down on me. God revealed to me it is my "Glory Ring".

October 21, 2006

My second vision was a water front with flowers at the shore. I walked out a little way and I saw Jesus standing on a cloud above me. The rays shone so bright. That was when Jesus told me he is coming for his bride and many feet a dancing.

October 21, 2006

The third vision was with Jesus and my-self. I caught a big fish and Jesus told me to pray for the fish. I did and then I released it. We went to the shore and as we were getting out of the boat, Jesus told me I will give you many blessing and I will give you the keys of the Earth.

March 18, 2007

The Holy Spirit told me the ring I got from work is, "My Glory Ring" and I should wear it to church every time I go. The Holy Spirit told me, we will have covenant love and marriage with Him.

January 25, 2008

I got up at 8:00 a.m. and I looked out the window. The Lord had made a masterpiece out of the frost we had just had. This brought so much joy and happiness to me. Later on we were driving west of the city where the field was so white and full of frost. This is when the Holy Spirit was telling me how white the Harvest is and said, "I want you to bring in the lost souls".

Later that day, I went to the dollar store and while I was there, the manager ran out of small bills. He trusted me enough to go to the bank and bring back change. He didn't know me and I didn't know him.

February 11, 2008

On this morning I went to the 9:00 a.m. mass. The priest anointed my hands and forehead with Holy Oil. When I went back to the bench I could feel my right hand heat up and I could feel the Lord Jesus' hand put the sign of the cross on my forehead.

June 1, 2008

I got up at 2:00 a.m. because I could not fall asleep. So I started to pray. That was when the Holy Spirit started to talk to me. He told me I have one sin in me. If I do not overcome this sin, everythingthat He had given to me would be takenfrom me. He also said whatever I put my hands to will come true. He will do a miracle in the lives of my wife, my son, my daughter and my mother-in-law.

September 19 to 21, 2008

I was at the McCoy High School "live-in" on September 19, 2008. Pat was praying at the front of the room and mentioned the foot of the cross. That is when the Holy Spirit told me to put that one sin at the foot of the cross. He saidHe will take away the sin, so I did.

On the morning of September 21, I opened my eyes and had freedom from that sin. I took the cross and put it on me and followed Jesus.

When I went back bible study, I was given a bible and they put this date,

September 19, 2000, inside it. That was when the Lord Jesus put me on a journey for eight years for total "freedom". I went to the "live-in" in Medicine Hat eight years later on the date September 19, 2008 and my journey was completed.

November 5, 2008

I went to the Sunny Side Care Centre for mass and Leo was praying the rosary. I had a vision. Virgin Mary was holding a book in her hands. I could see Psalms on the page. She was telling me to read the bible everyday.

February 20 to 22, 2009

I went to the "live-in", in Coaldale and in the morning of February 21, I got another vision. It was the Holy Spirit, raining down on the people. I was standing in the gym when a man told me there were three women that wanted to talk to me. I sat down and read to the three women, Psalms 91 and Ephesians 6:10 to 20, the Armor of God over them. I was drunk with the Holy Spirit. I left the gym and went to the hallway and met a woman. I told her I was filled with the Holy Spirit and I put my hand on her shoulder. As I did this, she was filled with the Holy Spirit also and fell down to the floor. There she laid, laughing fullof the Holy Spirit.

Orville H

Thank you Jesus for Leadingand Guiding Me

Miracle 16

My Special Son

God has always been a part of my life as far back as I can remember. I could not imagine surviving this life without a Higher Power sustaining me.

There has been many miracles in my life, the most recent one being January 7, 2008, when my special son was at the Medicine Hat Public Library. Jordan was sitting listening to music when he decided to go and look over the railing to see where his worker went downstairs. He lost his balance and fell to the basement floor (which is cement). He was still conscious and the first words he spoke were "Don't tell mom".

The Paramedics came quickly and took him to Emergency.

I know 'someone" helped to cushion his fall of 20 feet, because he could have sustained greater injuries than a black eye and a broken wrist.

Doris B.

Mother/Homemaker

Miracle 17

Ask and Ye Shall Receive

God has a sense of humor!

A good friend of mine, almost like a sister to me once suggested to me to be specific in Prayer. So this is how I set about a certain request to God. I made a list for a prospective husband listing the qualities I expected and wanted mostly in my husband. Some where as follows:

1) Either he had long hair or bald,

2) He stood 5'6" or taller and into fitness,

3) I was hoping he would have some class although not classy,

4) He needed to LOVE hockey like me,

5) But mostly he needed to be a very strong Christian Believing man.

After petitioning my Heavenly Father with my exact list of qualities, I was very happy to receive a beautiful gift of love. Less than two months later my Good Lord, Jesus sent me a beautifully bald headed "Pastor". To make a sweet, tender, loving story short, six months later we were married and he met all of the above noted traits above.

Let me also add that my sister also married a "Pastor" and we didn't come from a family of Believers! Do you believe in "Miracles"? I do!

Louise

Daughter, Mother, Friend and Wife

Miracle 18

The Right Green Glasses

A couple of years ago, something quite amazing happened to me when I decided to buy a new pair of glasses.

It had been about three years since I bought new glasses and early in August of that year, I felt compelled to buy a new pair. For some reason I had always bought reddish colored frames but now I felt I would definitely like to purchase a green pair. In my head I knew exactly what design I was looking for. First of all I wanted to find a good sale price, because glasses are so expensive for my thick lenses. Then I knew they had to be a forest green. I wanted them rectangular, plastic and open framed on the bottom.

I proceeded to look at frames within eye glass stores but found nothing. There were no frames like what I wanted.

I went for my eye exam and as I was leaving the doctors exam room, I again felt compelled to ask the doctor if their eye glass office had any discontinued frames available. Previously I had searched their stores general supply but found nothing.

Surprisingly when I questioned the doctor for discontinued eyewear, he replied: "We do have a few. Check with the clerk behind the glasses desk". As instructed, I said thank you and proceeded towards the young staff at the order desk. There on the doctor's suggestion I asked the young man if he had any discontinued frames available. He promptly replied, "Yes, we do. I'll get them."

He left the counter, went into his office and lab and returned to me in a couple moments carrying a medium sized wooden container. Before he opened it he asked me what design I had in mind. I explained, "Forest green, rectangular and open bottomed."

Now as a Believer I know God's word says: Ask and ye will receive; knock and it will open; seek and ye will find; and again God's Holy Word was proven to me to be truth!

Within seconds of describing exactly what I wanted, he opened the wooden box. I looked in and my eyes fell directly on the exact frame description I had just asked for!

I picked up the open bottomed, Forest Green, rectangular frames and somehow I knew God wanted me to have my hearts eye glass desire. They were also half price with no warranty and were also discontinued.

The young man was, for a moment, quite speechless because, neither he nor I knew those exact frames were hidden inside that special wooden box, but God did. Actually, I believe that Jesus may have put them there, possible moments before we looked in. Only God knows for sure.

For the last three years I have worn those frames happily with no manufactures problems and hope to wear them a long time yet. Thank you, Jesus. Your Word is Truth!

Again, God had worked another miracle! Thank you, Jesus!

Lana

Daughter, Auntie, Sister,
Mother and Wife

Miracle 19

A Rainbow on a Cloudy Day

It was John, my new husband, mom's funeral and for some reason I prayed for a nice day and a rainbow. The day came and it was overcast and there certainly was no rainbow to view. I was amongst some mourning family members when I voiced my concerns of the sky and no rainbows. John's son was present, heard my negative statement, and replied to me, "Look at that headstone!"

The name on it read "Rainbow". Well again, "Ask and Ye Shall Receive". It wasn't exactly what I had prayed for, but there it was, "A Rainbow".

Louise

A Believer

Miracle 20

World War II, 1945

Germany lost the war. All the German people in Poland were ordered to flee. For the fall of 1944, the Russians were coming closer and we Germans were told, "Prepare for the worst".

A wagon was made ready with a good cover with a pair of good horses and it was set, it could be anytime and we would have to leave. The last Christmas was celebrated very quickly. Even we children felt that the happiness was not there.

January the 6th, 1945, the bad news hit us. Our major went from house to house, and told everybody that in 24 hours we had to leave. Bedding, warm cloths and food were loaded on the wagon with two sacks of oats for the horses. Then 6 kids and Mother were helped on the wagon. My oldest brother

Erich and Dad had to stay back to fight the last battle.

We parted with hugs, tears and hoping that we would stay alive and some day come together again. Adolf our second oldest brother, 12 years old, and Stevka, our polish maid would trail the horses and follow the wagon-train.

It was 4 p.m. We got on the highway. There was no beginning and no endto all of the wagons. Coming towards us were big tanks and trucks with soldiers coming to fight the Russians back. Around 6 p.m. it got dark and we children fell asleep.

But shortly before midnight the tragedy happened. It was cold the highways were very icy and slippery. One horse slipped and pulled the wagon over the edge. Our wagon started to slide down the hill. It was very rough. Finely we stopped. Our cover was crumbled and our belongings had fallen off. We children were all over the place. Mom started to call our names. One by one was located, only one missing was our baby brother. He was 9 months old and not found yet.

Then Mom heard a whimper. She ran quickly and there he was, the baby. He had kicked all the blankets off and was ice cold. Mom quickly put him under her coat to warm him up. Now we huddled all on one pile and all were crying.

Who would ever find us here? It was pitch dark and cold. Then Adolf said to us, "Stay all here and keep each other warm. I will run for help."

But with war, going back to the highway, nobody would stop or even see him. Then a voice told him to look around. He then saw a light and started to run towards it.

We were scared that Adolf could get lost but I heard Mom cry and pray. Then the miracle happened.

Adolf got to the light. It was a German police station. He quickly explained what had happened. The policeman came with Adolf to us. He put us on the wagon and drove us back to the station.

It was nice and warm there but we still were crying.

We were badly bruised and Moms right-hand wrist was broken. Our little brother's chest was frozen. We got a little to eat while the man fixed our wagon. The police man put a few blankets and pillows on and told us to follow them back in the wagon-train.

My Mother insisted to turn around and go back home. Then the police told her, "Mrs. Werner, you can not do that. You will fall right in the enemy's hands and you all will be killed". Then Mom brought all of us children together and we moved on.

Without a cover it was much colder and we snuggled even more together. Mom's arm hurt badly. My oldest sister, Ella, cradled the baby and fed him his bottle.

Once a day we would stop near a village. The horses needed a rest and we had to go to the outhouse. Stevka would run from house to house and beg for food. Meanwhile Adolf would try to get some feed for the horses.

Bad weather came with rain and snow. Our blankets were soon wet. Now it was really cold. A couple days later we started to get sick. We got sore throats and the coughing started. We did not know how long this would last. After a couple day, our coughs got worse.

Then Mom said, "Children if we don't get help soon, we can't make it". She didn't want to scare us of dying and that's when God's help came again.

Our leader from our wagon-train stopped a number of wagons and said to us, "We are far ahead from the Russians. The have been pushed back. In one hour we will get to a village called "Ball". Here we will stay for a few days. And every family has been assigned a place were they can stay".

We must have gotten the nicest place. A lady opened the door and welcomed us in her house. It was nice and warm. We must have looked terrible, because she started to cry and said, "You poor children". She brought all kinds of clothes. We changed and now we were at least dry.

After a little while she gave each of us a cup of warm milk with honey. We sipped it very slowly. We had not tasted, for a long time any thing so good. Then she brought food and snacks. But we were so tired. She had straw mattresses laid out on the floor with lots of blankets. The night sleep was a tough one because we coughed and cried with pain. The next day we all had a warm bath, some more good food and we felt our bodies alive again.

Mom, Stevke and the lady washed our clothes and blankets. Meanwhile a few older men put a strong tarp on our wagon. After the 6 day stop-over, we moved on again.

I forgot the ladies name but she was our Angel. She gave us lots of food, blankets and clothes. Our colds were just about gone and we moved on. Now our wagon was nice and warm.

As we came closer to West Germany we felt safer. We could stop more often and get food. The horses could rest more. Some nights we could sleep in shelters. There is one night I remember most. It was a dairy farm with a big barn. It was spread with clean straw. A few hundred people spent the night. There were mostly women with their children. We took our coats off to cover our selves with. We were nestled close together but we could all stretch out. This felt good, as it had been very cramped in the wagon.

We were told, we would get a good breakfast. After awhile we all felt really itchy. We were scratching until blood was coming out. Then we cried. It wasso terrible!

Mother said, "I am itching also. This place is full of lice".

Soon as the sun came up everybody left the place. We forgot about breakfast. Now we had a job killing lice. We would count who would kill the most. We madea game of it. After awhile we quit because the numbers got to high. We must have done well though because the itching quit and we had a good sleep.

Another four weeks of hunger and fear unfolded and then we reached our new home, Schussbel, which would be our new home for some time. It was March 9, 1945. The next day, March 10, 1945, my brother Adolf had his 13th birthday and he was also our hero!

Mother and all of us children had survived the big, dangerous journey. All we could do was thank our Heavenly Father for all of our miracles! Many thanks to God, for I have been given a long abundant life first as a daughter, then wife and now as a Grandma. Thank you Jesus, my Savior.

Oma,

Housewife and Believer

Miracle 21

My Little Brother's Polio Miracle

As I now write my story, I still can hardy believe the wonderful miracle our family received from God. It involved my brother (two years younger than I), who at the time was about four and a half years old. I vividly remember him, in my mother's arms, crying and pulling at his hair as the pain in his head became unbearable. He kept repeating, "Jei mal de tete", translated means, "My head hurts".

My Mom and Dad took him to the doctor who, on examination, diagnosed him with Infantile Paralysis and then had him hospitalized. The tests taken and sent to Edmonton came back as "positive for Poliomyelitis". The nuns, who at the time ran the hospital, informed us that my brother had no sensation in his limbs, even though they followed the "Sister Kenny" treatment on him. Every day a series of immersing of both legs in hot water, alternating with cold water were to no avail. He was paralyzed in both legs from the hips down. There was, at the time, no vaccination for this dreaded disease. Polio became an epidemic across the country during those early 1930's.

Our cousin, who lived on a farm some ten miles from ours, also became a victim of this scourge. She was left permanently paralyzed in one leg. Every year her shoes had to be specially fitted. As she grew, the sole of her shoe, on the afflicted limb, had to be heightened in order to make up its difference.

As our family realized the serious consequences resulting from this disease, our nightly family rosary became a petition to God for my brother's recovery. We knew that his recovery would take a 'miracle'. My Dad, who was what I'd call an addicted pipe smoker, gave up his tobacco for a whole year as a penance in supplication for my brother's recovery. My four older sister's who were teenagers, gave up all movies, dances, parties and all other social events for a year, following my Dad's example. Mom, who had just given birth to a baby sister, patiently endured a great deal of worry during those trying times. However she continued to believe, ever so faithfully, in the power of prayer.

I, at the young age of 6 ½, only knew that we had to seriously pray for my kid brother. Our prayers were joined by those of the nuns at the hospital and also by the prayers of the nuns at a convent in Quebec, where my Dad's sister was 'Mother Superior'.

Praise God! God did answer those prayers! In a short time, my brother regained the use of his legs and to this day you'd never guess that he ever had Polio. His legs grew normally and he is proof that "Miracles" do happen!

My Dad continued giving up his pipe of tobacco. My sisters and family attended no social events for the remaining balance of the year, keeping their promises to God. This was all done in a spirit of gratitude and thanksgiving.

Some people still questioned my brother's test results, saying perhaps an error was made and he could have had a case of Meningitis. Fourteen or fifteen years after the fact, one of my sisters was hired to work as a stenographer at the University of Alberta, in the Pathology Department. She decided to look up my brother's Medical File in order to put all doubts to rest. On doing so, what she read clearly stated, "Acute Poliomyelitis".

Sincerely,

M.R.C.F, Believer, Homemaker, and Grandmother

Miracle 22

Is this a (medical) miracle or (Miracle) Miracle?

I'm a 72-year-old male, happily married for 51 years with 4 wonderful children, 6 grandchildren and 1 great granddaughter. I was hard working and in good physical condition, running my own business. Everything was going fine, until 1972, when my health problems started. Lucky for us, that my wife and son worked with me and were able to operate the business, while I was unable to be fully active.

My problems began when I had to have my gall bladder removed at which time the doctor informed me that I had sugar diabetes. At the time I was unaware of my family history of diabetes, as I was orphaned at age 9 and raised outside the family. Even though I was always careful and mindful of the diabetes, it caused me to have a cardiac arrest in

July of 1988. I was told then that I was lucky to have survived without brain damage, but my heart was damaged, operating at 28% of its capability.

In April of 1989, I had further heart problems, at which time I had to have an angiogram and angioplasty. In November 1990, I had a stroke and my left side was totally paralyzed for the next three months and I lost my speech for 3 days. After 6/8 months of therapy I regained mobility with a walker, then a cane, and was able to drive again, after passing a medical driving test, 2 years later.

In October of 1994, I had a second major heart attack and was given the option of taking a once in a lifetime drug called Streptokinase and had 20 seconds to make my mind up, but the side effects were that it could cause hemorrhaging, but without it, I probably wouldn't survive, so I decided to take it and here I am. Was that another miracle?

In late October 1994, I was again given an angiogram which showed that there was an artery on the heart that was enlarged like an overblown bicycle tube and was hemorrhaging from it. No angioplasty required, doctor said it would heal itself, with time and medication.

In December of 1994 more heart problems, another angiogram done and an angioplasty which included a stent installed in one of my arteries.

In April of 1997 after unstable angina, I was given another angiogram. The doctor told me to go home and put my affairs in order, as there was nothing more they could do for me.

In June of 1997, I was flown back to Calgary for another angiogram and a heart scan which showed my heart was only operating at 24%. I was flown back home, no procedure done.

In November 1997, I was flown back to Calgary. At this time, a lady cardiac surgeon was assigned to me and informed me that I required quadruple bypass surgery, which could be extremely dangerous in my condition, but she would be willing to give me a chance, if I would take it. She said that if I didn't, I would probably survive for about a week. She said I wouldn't die on the operating table but after that, it would be between me and my God. Again, I had another success story, after a week of cardiac intensive care, thanks to a compassionate and devoted heart surgeon and the master above.

In June of 2007, I had circulation problems (caused by diabetes) in both legs at which time I was given angioplasty in my left leg, which helped me, get off my walking cane.

In November of 2007, I was taken off oral medication for diabetes and started using two different types of insulin, which seems to control the diabetes more accurately than the many medications I was taking previously.

In June of 2008, I was diagnosed with aggressive prostate cancer, because of my history it was decided the best form of treatment at this time, would be hormone pill therapy, which would be the least intrusive of the treatments available. So far, with that treatment, I've been good.

Another factor which should not be forgotten is the prayers and support of my family, friends and the community as a whole, who have been supporting me, through these years.

I thought I would share my story with you, so that if you have a serous medical problem, never give up. Positive attitude and finding humor in daily life, goes a long way in overcoming many problems. Never give up hope and put your faith in the Lord. Be close to family and friends. Follow your medical team's advice and their educated opinions. Once you've done all you can, enjoy each day that is given to you and count your blessings! Laugh each day and enjoy good living, one day at a time. May God bless us all!!!

A.A., Believer, Husband, and Father

Miracle 23

For every Season there is a Reason

When my adopted Mother was 29 she lost her second child who died inside of her. The doctors did not know until she nearly died. While in the hospital operating room she had an out of body experience. She saw herself going towards the light but an angel appeared and told her that her work on Earth was not finished. The angel was holding the hand of a little girl. Mom started to go more towards the light because she said it was so beautiful but the angel again said, "No, you have to go back to finish your work here on Earth.

Many years later they decided to adopt a child. When they went to the Adoption Agency to look at children they asked to see little girls. When they bought me in to be viewed Mom said that she knew right away that I was the one because she recognized that I was the little girl who was holding the hand of the angel.

Some people do not believe in out of body experiences but I do. Many times in life we can not understand why things happen the way they do, but if we have faith and believe then all things are possible with God.

Daughter, Wife, Mother and Believer

Y. E.

Miracle 24

The Believers Voice of Clarence

God is so kind and gracious. He gives us life and others to love us. He gives us every possible thing we can imagine. Much of the time we aren't even awareof His goodness.

And if that wasn't enough, He sent His Son to offer us life for all eternity. But it's not without sacrifice on our part.It is God's way or not at all. We cannot choose how to come to Him. He told us the way!

I want to tell you that you can have peace with God, but there is a choice tobe made here. You must decide what you want more, life your own way or lifeGods way.

God tells those who have trusted in Him to confess their sins and He forgives them every time. Even if old habits enter in, there is way to deal with those also.

What if I still might be afraid and have no peace. God will choose to take all fear and doubt away the moment you trust in His Son. What He does promise is to never give us more than we can bear nor leave us alone in any struggle. How can I be sure of all this?

Basically, we all choose to believe in something but if we choose to put out trust in the word of God, God is Faithful and He will prove Himself to us, over and over again! God loves you!Ask Jesus into your hearts, repent and know that God will never leave you norforsake you, no matter where you are inlife! God Bless You, Now and Eternally!

Clarence

One of God's Children

Miracle 25

My Miracle Testimony

On December 16, 2002, about 1:30am I awoke to find that I was unable to speak. All that would come out was a garbled sound. My right side had no feeling and try as hard as I could, I was unable to move my hand or arm. I knew what had happened – I had a stroke! I knew because my father had a stroke when I was about 10 – 11 and I knew how it had debilitated him. I knew this was serous and I knew I had to get help as fast as possible.

My wife awoke and I tried to tell what had happened. Not a word would come out. I pointed to the phone and showed her 911. I wanted her to call 911. She had just awakened from a sound sleep and I didn't seem to make sense to her. However she reached the phone and I pointed to 911 and in a moment the operator came on and Doris explained that I was sick. In a few minutes an ambulance was on the way. Doris went down to open the door and I was alone. That was when I sensed the Lord, as He spoke into my heart, "Do not be afraid, I will go through this with you". Instantly I knew that I had nothing to worry about and a peace come over me that was unshakable.

Then the Medics were beside the bed assessing the situation. How were they going to get this big man down the narrow stairway? With one Medic in front and one behind holding me up, I was able to make the steps, one at a time.

Soon I was on a bed in the Emergency and the doctor was checking me over. Then he addressed himself to my wife as if I wasn't there, telling her that I had had a stroke and that it was very bad. He thought that if I was lucky and with many months of therapy I might recover some use of my limbs and speech.

How I wished I could tell Doris what God had said and calm her fears. The most frustrating thing was not being able to speak. After a while I was moved to a room and put into a bed. At this point I was unable to move my right arm or leg or say anything intelligible. I tried writing notes but found I was unable to write legibly. I knew what I wanted to write but seemed that I didn't form the letters right.

As soon as my pastors heard, they rushed over to pray for me. As one prayed he read from the Psalms 41:1-3. As he read these verses, God witnessed that this was for me, confirming what He had said earlier.

Soon they had alerted the Church to pray for me and I was covered with a blanket of Prayer.

Much to the surprise of the Doctors and Nurses I began to recover. By evening I was able to wiggle my toes under the blankets. By Tuesday there was such a marked improvement they had trouble believing it and were starting to call it a miracle. I was able to make it to the bathroom with two nurses holding me to make sure I didn't fall. I could move my arm and leg but still lacked strength. I could speak some but was still garbled. By Thursday, I could speak clearly and my right side had regained most of its strength.

Visitors were welcome and my room was full as they came and went, disturbing the nursing staff, as they thought I should be resting. I felt great and was able to testify to all that came, about what God was doing. Wednesday and Thursday they did various tests, trying to determine what was happening and the extent of the damage. They were certain that I had suffered a massive stroke. They were also sure that I was recovering my functions at a rate they could not explain! The only explanation was that God was doing a miracle, which most of the staff agreed with.

On Friday morning I walked out of the hospital just 104 hours after I realized what was happening to me and when God gave me assurance that He was going to be with me through it all. I was able to walk and talk normally. Today, just one month later I am sitting at my computer typing this testimony. I have been doing most of what I had been doing before, just enough effects to keep me thanking God for His Mercy.

The above was written in January 2003. Today, April 7, 2009, I can still say that God did a miracle for me and He continues to sustain me day by day. There are no visible effects of the strokeon December 16, 2002.

Ernest Murschel

Believer in Jesus Christ
and the Holy Trinity

Miracle 26

Miracle Baby

It was a beautiful sunny day, a Sunday in July 1955. My late husband, Harvey and I decided to go and visit his Aunt and Uncle who lived out in the country. Away we went with our daughter Linda, who at the time was 14 months old. We were anticipating a lovely day which turned into a nightmare.

After dinner I helped with the dishes,I then decided to sit on the patio outside to rock Linda for her afternoon nap. I was four months pregnant at that timealso.

Out in the front yard Harvey's cousin was working on his car. He decidedto try and drive it to see if the brakes were working. They failed and the car hit the patio with such force that Lindaflew out of my arms over the banister unto the ground. Her dress got caught onto the front bumper of the car. She was dragged away before a relative ran towards the car to stop the car.

In the meantime, I flew off the rocking chair onto the floor of a cement patio and passed out. When I came to, a cousin of Harvey was kneeling beside me and with her two hands was pushing down on my belly to hold my baby down, as it was pushing its way up into my esophagus. She kept pushing until the doctor arrived. He gave Linda and me a needle for shock. The he wrapped some material around my chest in order for me to breathe better.

After examining me, he told me I was going to carry my baby the full 9 months. He bandaged the back of my leg that got ripped open by a piece of board. As you can see I was in bad shape. The lady who was beside me, when I came to, said that my face had turned blue. Linda and I were taken to the hospital in Cornwall, Ontario. Linda was released from the hospital after one week so her Grandpa Guindon looked after her, as I was in the hospital for two weeks.

It was a nightmare I was not going to forget too soon! After that accident, when we went for car rides, I had to lie down on the back seat, as I could not stand to see any on-coming cars coming towards us.

After one year, I finally sat in the front seat. As miracles do happen, my baby boy was born on December 2, 1955, in perfect shape. I was afraid that he might have some injuries. We named him Aubrey, after a friend of Harvey's and he is alive and well, living in Calgary with his wife Cathy. Aubrey has two adult children living in Ontario, Aaron and Amy. Aubrey and Cathy are Grandparents to Joshua and Nayla.

God is a God of Miracles

Anita Guindon

A note to ponder: The reason for the title "Miracle Baby," is that after Aubrey was born, Raymond was born on August 4, 1957 and died on that same day of R.H. Factor and on August 19, 1959, Helen was born and died on that same day of R. H. Factor. Thank you, God, for my two living babies and for the two that went home to be with Jesus. My two surviving children are truly "Miracle" children and are a true testimony of God's Grace. Thank you, Father! Anita.

Miracle 27

A Few of our own Miracles

Dale, our second son, was born with blood AO incompatibility. He needed a complete blood exchange or transfusion, immediately, just to live. However, my husband and I were church going Christian's and had asked our church members to pray for our baby.

Within ten days of birth, somehow our son's blood AO incompatibility resolved itself. By the Grace of God, no transfusions were necessary. Dale, our new son and I came home healthy and well!

The day my husband took me to give birth at the hospital, the June landscape was dry and brown. On returning home just ten days later, the grass was green from abundant rain!

Praise God for His Miracles! And thank you Jesus for our little boy's good health.

Years later our son Dale, well and healthy, met his future wife, Lisa while working at a Christian camp. Both Lisa and Dale were on staff. A short time later Lisa and Dale got married in Calgary. There marriage was blessed with two little girls.

On December 19, 2003, Tobi was born and the very following February, early in the month, Dale, her daddy went skiing with a group of students he taught at school. While they were on the hill an enormous avalanche swept all the skiers, 12 children and 4 adults, down one side of a mountain and up onto another mountain.

Dale's thoughts were of his family. When the avalanche had settled, Dale was buried to his waist. He dug himself out and helped dig out another staff member who had a phone.

Help was called via satelite telephone. All the adults survived but seven children didn't. With such a horrendous huge impact it was and is considered a miracle that Dale and the others survived.

Since this terrible happening our son has been led to start a bible study and prayer time for the men of the school and community. Our son painfully remembers that terrible day in the mountains but gratefully thanks God, his Father in Heaven, for a second chance of life. It has not diminished his true love of the mountains and appreciated God's glorious creation.

Miracle Baby in White

Garry, our first son, wanted to be a R.C.M.P. so he took two years of law and enforcement in Lethbridge, Alberta. Finally Garry became a bylaw officer in Bow Island, Alberta. Many times on duty he had "radar" equipment placed on his lap ready for usage.

Garry, also believed in God and attended Southview Church of God with us, his parents. This is where Garry met a Christian girl that had also previously attended Bible College. The two young Believers fell in love and decided to set a date to get married.

After the wedding date was set, Garry continued to fill his duties as Bylaw officer in Bow Island and continued with the "radar" equipment. In the month of May, Garry was hospitalized while his wedding date was set for September 1, which was in a few short months down the road. In the hospital he learned that he had cancer in his pelvic area. Garry asked us, his parents, to call Lois, his wife to be, and let her know of his situation.

Garry had surgery and three rounds of Kemo. He lost all his hair. We found out later that Lois's friends had advised Lois to stop the relationship with Garry because of the severe Cancer. His doctor's said that the young couple would never be able to have children because of the extensive Kemo but Lois decided to listen to her heart and marry the man of her dreams in spite of any possible Cancer complications. The date came and they were married September1, only months after Garry's illness.

Now at that time also, Garry had a friend that had committed suicide and this friend's mother made hair wigs for patience, like Garry, with Cancer. This lady styled Garry's mothers, only wig to fit Garry for the months of doctoringand then also for their wedding.

By the Grace of God, Jesus has been active in their lives for 18 years of married life to each other and also is Cancer FREE! Blessing upon blessing, they also have two beautiful children by birth. We, Garry's parents and our children, Garry and Lois, Praise our Living Savior, Jesus.

When Garry and Lois conceived and had their first child, they had a beautiful little girl. However, miracles were happening because not only did they conceive a child but as the nurses and hospital staff were cleaning up baby,

Janine, they were all very amazed at the "white" light surrounding their little infant. All present in the delivery room felt a definite presence, before and after the birthing. Mother and child were well. Again, we thank our Holy Father and His Precious Son

Miracle 28

Personal House Miracles

We farmed 1 and ½ miles west of Elkwater turnoff by #1 highway. In spring we would many times get flooded from spring runoff of Elkwater Lake and this was one of those times.

We called and asked our Pastor Mel to pray for salvage and help for our home. Within an hour or so, there on the yard's waterfront came Pastor Mel in a boat, looking to help. While we were standing on the step of the house, the water level visably was rising right in front of us. We asked Pastor Mel to pray and agreeing he prayed, sending a callof help up to a God that hears every prayer.

Within moments it leveled off! It stopped rising! Praise God!

About a day or so later, we found out how come the water stopped rising. It had broken out of the creek in a different place and went down the other side of the highway. Our home was saved! To God be the Glory!

Marlene and Clarence,

Believers and Children
of God's Kingdom

Miracle 29

My Nieces Miracle

A young mom of 38 years old had lots of headaches. She went to doctors every 2 or 3 months about her bad migraines. They said to take Tylenol Three, so she did. At first it helped a bit, but later it didn't. A year or so went by and her arm went paralyzed. The doctors arranged an MRI for her on her head.

There showed a tumor. They immediately sent my young niece to Calgary to check tumor for Cancer. There the doctors found it to be Cancer and as large as an egg. Immediately Calgary doctors operated trying to remove the tumor.

They removed most of it but, one little piece of it was left inside her. She was given Kemo therapy and that was said to be successful. A year passed and the terrible tumor started to grow back. Another operation was done in

Calgary and this time was completely successful.

Within a month of the second, which was successful, operation, my niece started bleeding in her brain and the headaches started again. She was able to come and stay at the Medicine Hat Regional Hospital for awhile but then she had to return to the Foothills Hospitalin Calgary.

Within a few days the doctors called the family together. My niece was in a coma and was expected to live until the end of the day. This is where the miracle came in.

My brother went over to his daughter, kissed her cheek to say goodbye and all of a sudden her eyes popped open and she replied, "Dad they sent me backagain. You wanted me back here". The doctor came in that evening to check onmy niece to see if she was still alive. She greeted the doctor with conversation.

The doctor was amazed! He was surehe was witnessing a miracle because he couldn't understand it!

Her family, too, were all amazed at her wellness!

For three weeks my niece received treatment in Calgary and then she was released to go to her home. There she resided for about three to four months. After four months at home with her children and family she started getting headaches again.

She returned to her doctor about her return of headaches and he immediately admitted her back in Medicine Hat Regional Hospital. There my sweet niece started to get more migraines.

After a month of suffering, she passedon because of a blood clot at the tenderage of 40 years old. The observation from the doctors was that she did not die from Cancer but the actually from the operation on her head.

From the time the doctors said in Calgary that she would die that day, she actually was well enough to live for about another six months.

God gave my special niece an extra 6 months to be with us here on earth. I believe my very loving Niece, Sandra is well, healthy and vibrant up in Heaven with Jesus and her mother, looking down to us and all of her family! I would just like Sandra to know that we love her and one day we will reunite in Jesus' Name!

Margaret,

Sister,

Auntie, And Child of God

Miracle 30

My Dear Brother

Hi Friends, I need to share this with you as members of the Legion of Mary.

On Saturday, I consecrated myself to Our Blessed Mother and Queen. Today, I received a phone call from my brother, Joe. He lives in Vancouver. He is the black sheep of the family. Before he was born my mother prayed for a boy and promised to name him Joseph.

Last week on St. Joseph's feast day, I was going to call him and I forgot. My brother dabbles in all religions and experiences, etc. I told him he should be a priest one time. He is divorced and has two sons (15 and 9). He works on the railroad for CN in Vancouver.

Anyway, needless to say, he does not go to church. He has read a lot of new age junk and particularly Eckart

Tolle. He does not watch television. He is studying the mystics and some other stuff (I could not talk to him for long because I had company). But yesterday, he was downtown and he saw someone who looked exactly like me when I was 21. He was so startled! He has also been getting visions of our great grandmother who died about 20 years ago. He was never close to her (I was very close to her and spent a lot of time with her). I had showed my brother our great grandmother's rosary about 2 years ago.

He held it in his hand until it started to burn him! Yes, it was burning his hand. Now that he is getting this vision of Granny Duffy (that is what we called her because our grandmother was called Nanny), and then he sees someone who looks like me, he puts together that he should phone me!!! As soon as he explains what is happening I realized that it was the consecration to Our Lady that is now working in him. I told him I would send him the rosary and that he could start praying it. I mailed it about half an hour ago!!!

I had to share this with you because he phoned right while you were having your Legion of Mary meeting because Helen phoned me right after!

So Our Lady is working a lot and sometimes we do not see it but it is happening!

Then I got a call today from the Wilsons (Bob and Rosalee from Brooks). Father John had been giving them rave reviews about the Bible Study and they want to know about it.

So, sisters, keep doing what you are doing – Our Lady is working in the parish and outside of it.

God Bless,

Cathy

Miracle 31

A Drug Addict for Four Years

Here is a summary of what my life held in a daily, monthly, yearly way. I was addicted to Cocaine for four years and out of any control of my life. My whole life was focused on drugs, dealing, getting and ingesting. I was a musician and full of drugs. I don't know how I was able, but the money cost of this lively-hood, was extreme. I spent daily any where from $300.00 to $800.00 for my deathly habit.

I had married quite young and had been married for a few years but that didn't work out. We separated and divorced while shortly after the separation I started doing drugs. My, choice of drugs were, marijuana, cocaine and alcohol. Very soon, after starting, I was addicted, and nothing else seemed important to me. Nothing else mattered! Soon I had to have all the above to function at all. I wasn't even able to make a simple phone call with out a fix. I was only able to go to sleep with promising myself more drugs in the morning.

I soon wasn't working anymore and was hanging around drug dealers with drugs always available. Sometimes the drugs were worked for or free.

At the end of the fourth year, paranoia set in and I thought I was losing my mind. I thought I was being watched and I was always very suspicious of everyone. Normal relationships were impossible. I thought no one loved me anymore.

I had been sitting on the fence about believing in God and I, though God was the last personal resource for me to turn to. I was very delusional with the practice of magic and my style of living. I was hurting badly and thought I would just one day take to much drugs and just expire.

I was displaying suicidal symptoms and giving personal things away that I considered valuable to me. Everything had lost its value except drugs. I was not able to sustain my word or promises at all. As I was coming to the end of this physical and mental, self abuse, I was also using pharmaceutical drugs.

Then one, almost, deathly day, I took an overdose after two sleep deprived nights. I had taken extra drugs, then, the convulsions and asphyxiation started. I was looking at literally minutes and seconds of my life left.

My last living breath is when God stepped in. When there was no one else, I asked God verbally, "God, if you exist, this is your chance." As I pushed out these desperate words, the dying condition abated, stopped and I fell asleep, finally.

During this time also, a few of my friends called my sister about my abuse. A few days after the dying experience, my father came to me and asked, "Will you come with me to Pilgramioria Meduguje", which is in Bosnia, Eastern Europe. That is where Virgin Mary appears to six people still, to this day. I jumped up and said, "Yes!" I didn't really understand what this all meant, but I really wanted to go there!

We started planning the trip. I was still on drugs. My passport picture looks like me propped up and dead. However, I started making my own plans. I had plans of ditching my parents and then partying, once I got there.

The night before we left Canada, I bought drugs and stayed up most of the night. The next morning I was up at 7:00, with my packed suitcase. I actually don't remember packing it at all. I just remember being in Moms and Dads car with my perfectly packed suitcase.

The moment I got into Dads car, I felt like I was not addicted to drugs anymore, which was very strange. I felt that I had permanently damaged my brain, by how slow I was mentally and physically. I thought I was permanently handicapped.

When we got to Europe, officials asked, "Are you ok?" Most of the rest of the trip was standard. We got into a small town and something inside of me changed drastically. My heart was opening emotionally to God. From that point on, I couldn't stop walking and talking to priests in the confessional. I made my first confession to a priest in 15 years.

Something changed again! I became, again, more open to take in more of this experience.

The leader of the Pilgrimage prayed over me. I thought, "Wow, freaky". I didn't want anything to do with that. But Mom and Dad were sitting close by me, so I got up into line. I put my hands in my pockets as a type of defiance and I was afraid that maybe I might fall down under the Spirit of God.

My turn came. He didn't touch me, but he prayed and put his hand up over and towards my head. I went down! I experienced Great Peace and rested for about two minutes under the power of the Spirit of God.

Something changed again! My very basic brain function was changing. I was becoming more focused and more peaceful. I was also becoming more clearly aware.

Soon it was day two of our trip. AfterI got up, I readied myself and literally ran to God in a hurry, like a baby, in ability. I went to a 30 foot statue of Jesus Christ and realized that I didn't know how to pray.

I, and everyone else, was seeing that the statue of solid bronze was weeping from the knee and had been for many years. I touched the liquid with my hand and anointed my head. I found out that the liquid is made of human tears substance and that the statue, of Jesus, is made of solid bronze!

I was given the desire to pray! I sat there not knowing how to pray. I thoughtto pray the Rosary because of Mother Mary. I went back to my room to pray.

I ended up writing out the Rosary and went back to the statue. There I prayed for 3 or 4 hours, always making mistakes and starting over. I was very naive.

Even feeling so well, I probably could not go home and stay clean. At that point I knew I was to stay longer, perhaps a year. I started looking for a place to live, perhaps the rehab place. I found the rehab centre and the Priest said I could stay three weeks to three years.

At the end of the pilgrimage I told my parents that I was staying longer. I was there for three weeks. I was in culture shock within the community. Other people were left there as lost luggage. I didn't feel like I belonged there. I asked if I could leave. I went back to Majadoria and stayed another week in rehab. There, I learned the Rosary, said own little prayers, and went to mass daily while not realizing my growth and healing in my spirit and body.

Soon it was time to go home to Canada and there I received a warm welcome and reception. I had mentally, physically, and emotionally gone a complete 180 degrees change of direction in my life. A Priest, that my parents knew, recommended counseling for healing to get through the rest of my journey. Through Christians and counseling, I learned all about myself and how to deal with life.

Over the next year I probably went to mass every day. I found it necessary to go daily and receive the Eucharist to maintain my spiritual path and to continue healing.

Through counseling I learned that becoming a Priest may be my calling. After a year of counseling I moved to a near by farm to live by myself in solitude. Two years went by and people started to say that I should go to work but basically all I knew how to do was to play drums. So I contacted previous band mates and started playing gigs again, three or four nights a week. I did NOT drink!

Over time, however, I fell back into drinking. I realized I was backsliding with alcohol progressing.

I met a girl at one of our gigs who had a son. Everything seemed perfect except she was not a Christian.

At the same time I had planned another pilgrimage to Mejorgia to reinforce my faith. On one of the nights there, people were invited to a Public Apparition. At the apparition, I heard actual words from Heaven that said, "Take her boy to church".

When I went back to Canada that is exactly what I did. I started taking both girl and son with me to church. Shortly afterward she wanted to become Catholic. Her son followed shortly after, as well, with the same decision.

I took another Pilgrimage with out her, only to find that we missed each other terribly. On arrival back to Canada, we overstepped our boundaries and conceived a child. Meeting this young woman and child basically gave me a new purpose in my life. We got married, have a beautiful baby girl, a wonderful young son, a purpose and a life FULL of LOVE with the love of my life, wife.

Thank you, Jesus, Father God and Holy Spirit, for I would have died, missed out on true love and suffered in Hell, if You were not my Savior! Thank you, Precious Holy Trinity, for resurrecting my life!

Son, Husband, Father

And Believer

In the Almighty, Father God

Who Saved MY Life

Who Now, I Put My Faith In

Miracle 32

My Family

When I see my children and their families, I feel I am blessed, as I see the struggles that so many other families have and also what I have overcome, personally.

Our young life as a married couple started out rocky and unsure. Because of family dysfunctions on both sides of our family lives, we really didn't understand how to make a functioning family life for us and our children. Because of the need for a job, we made a choice to move about 500 miles from home. Neither of us, ever having left home from childhood, left our home town at twenty and twenty-four years young, not knowing a soul where we were going.

When my husband, child and I left home, it was for the sake of survival of our relationship and employment. I have always believed in Devine Providence and I believe we were meant to be in Redcliff, Alberta.

We found a basement suite. This spring it will be 37 years since we moved to this town of Alberta and our family is a Christian walking and trusting, children and grandchildren, family. We were blessed with two more children, another son and a daughter, in the next three years after moving here.

Six weeks before we moved out here, both of us came here for one official job interview, for my husband, and to look for a home to live in. The most difficult thing for me, was meeting other people, as I was always very shy. I was very lucky to be a stay at home mom. My husband and I had different denominations and thus difficulties deciding which church to attend.

Through Devine intervention, my husband agreed to attend the Catholic Church with me. He took instruction from the Catholic Church and we had our marriage blessed. As time went on,

I at times felt that he was a stronger Christian than I was. Our children were all baptized and taken regularly to church. There was never any question about or Sunday Mass routine. Our children, with us, grew up in a Bible believing home with the Bible as our guide.

Shortly after we moved here, some of my husbands brothers and sisters moved close by. Over the years, all of them lived here. They lived a different life style than us and at times, we were chastised because of our Christian lifestyle and beliefs.

My childhood family, despite being somewhat dysfunctional, supported us emotionally from a distance. Whenever they visited, they would try to help us out. I think over the years, the distance physically put between my mom and dad and us kids, actually brought us closer together. For that, I am very grateful!

As years went by, our children grew, teen years and all, but there never was, any serious issues like my husband's young family life. The previous dysfunctions that we knew of with-in our family were actually disappearing and our lives were growing into a beautiful Christian experience, with our beautiful children.

The previous generation of dysfunction was being broken and our children were growing into wonderful, healthy, successful adults. Thank you, Jesus!

Despite an uphill struggle financially, God was the glue in our family that held us together by faith! Our children have learned the value of a dollar and know money has to be worked for.

On one of our Christmases, due to the economy situation, we struggled with finances and Christmas looked barren. I was a worrier and I knew God was there with us, but in my human weakness, I wondered why he helped others financially and not us.

Going to bed in the middle of December, totally drained from financial worry, I begged for a restful sleep to clear my thick mind of the worry. As I closed my eyelids the blackness disappeared and I saw a silvery whiteness and felt comforting, internal warmth. With-in moments I fell fast asleep! In the morning I felt like I had slept a week and the worry was gone!

Christmas unfolded nicely. We had a Charlie Brown Christmas tree with a few gifts under it. It was one of the simplest yet most beautiful Christmas times we ever enjoyed as a family. We had food, gifts, were healthy and had each others company. Thank you, Jesus!

As the years went by, maybe the last ten years or so, I have come to realize that our family relationships are loving and special, including two wonderful daughters-in-law and one wonderful son-in-law. Also included in our family so far are five precious grandchildren. We truly are blessed!

The generational dysfunctions, praise God, has been broken!

My husband and I are on our own now as our children are grown. We still have financial element concerns within our life but I have learned that Jesus is always in charge, and His Devine Providence will always supply what we need. Financially we may not be millionaires but, by the Grace of God, we are grounded spiritually, like a family of millionaires.

Some years ago, I attended women's aglow at a friends coaxing. At that meeting I was given a scripture passage from Jeremiah. The passage stated – Not to worry about my kids. They were all in there early teens at the time and this scripture was an answer to my prayers.

Another friend also told me that at night when she went to sleep, she would ask God to watch over her children. As she watched them all day, she felt Jesus could watch them at night and when ever they were not around her. I started to do the same thing and that took a lotof pressure off of my mind.

Struggles, with our oldest son being away at University, often worried us because we were not able to go visit him that often. Later he told us that he had done a lot of praying over and through that three year period.

Since then he has met and married a wonderful young woman, that at first didn't know Jesus but as God had intended, they are now a God loving and believing family, blessed with two beautiful children.

Our younger son was our biggest prayer challenge, as he was looking for a compatible companion, also. It always seemed girls he met were the wrong ones, for different reasons. After the last disappointing relationship he was very down. As his parents, my husband and I joined in prayer power. We petitioned to Jesus to send someone just right for our lonely, discouraged son.

As God IS Faithful, by the Grace of God, our now daughter-in-law came onto the scene. She is everything our son loves in a companion plus God sent him, and us, a beautiful Christian lady, to further and deepen our families' foundation. Thank you, Jesus, for answered prayer.

With God's blessing pouring into our family, we have recently been blessed again with a beautiful Grandson, to love and enjoy from this loving couple.

Our youngest and only daughter struggled with peer pressure in her pre-teen years. Then we gave her the opportunity to change schools. The summer before she attended high school, our daughter attended Camp McCoy with a childhood friend. While she was at camp she met a lot of new sincere friends. Her high school years were probably her best school years ever. Those years built her self esteem and self worth.

Sometime in grade 12, she met her new friend and husband to be, through one of her friends. Two years later they were married and were blessed with two wonderful children. Over the years she has become very strong in her faith which reflects throughout her daily living.

I would just like to say, "Thank you, God for all you have accomplished in our lives!" Thank you for our family foundation that is so vibrant, loving and God centered. Amen.

We have travelled from dysfunctional living to" Blessed" in Every Way!

Glory to the Living Savior
God Almighty

A Believer in Your Promises

Sharon

Miracle 33

Eye Problem

I am asking and believing Jesus for a Miracle for my eyes. And this is why.

My husband and I, a few years ago, went south for the winter months. I was continually in pain with sore eyes with no type of relief available. While sitting outside, late one afternoon, along the sidewalk, it started to get dark. As people passed by, something out of the ordinary happened! All of a sudden a stranger, middle aged with grey hair, was walking past us and spoke these words to, it seemed, me. "Don't give up hope. Things will get better!"

I looked at my husband in a bit of shock and asked him if he had heard the words of the encouragement also. My husband said, "Yes, I did!"

Both my husband and I had an odd light feeling and wonder if that person was really a stranger or was it possibly a guardian angle. With renewed encouragement and hope, I am waiting for Jesus to heal my painful eyes, for His Word says, "By His stripes we are healed!" We only have to accept His Promises and they are ours. Thank you, my Personal Savior and Almighty God!

By the Hand of God

We are "Saved"

And made Whole

J. M.

Miracle 34

In God's Hands

"The Angel of the Lord encamps around you." Psalm 91:11

"For He gives, His Angels, orders to protect you wherever you go." (L.B)

What had started out to be an ordinary Saturday morning suddenly turned into a battle to save our son's right eye. I told him to lie down and rest his eyes for a few minutes. Returning four to five minutes later, I could see by the anxious and painful look on his face that all was not well. Upon looking at his eye, I immediately said a quick prayer. The retina had suddenly turned bright red, an indication of serious injury.

After I'd checked Kent's eye, I scooted a few steps to the garage where my husband was working and asked him to look in Kent's eye as well. His advice was that I'd better call the doctor. I dialed our local city hospital and the doctor on call informed me that the eye had hemorrhaged due to a retinal injury and we needed to get Kent to the hospital as soon as possible. On the way to the hospital, Kent had become very anxious, fearing he would lose the sight of his eye. (Keep in mind that the eyes of a deaf person compensate for their hearing loss, providing a sixth sense.) I tried to comfort him, reminding him that God was looking after him, but to no avail. Finally arriving at the hospital and following the doctor's observation, he confirmed that Kent would require a four to five day stay in a darkened room with his eyes blind-folded.

For Kent, the feeling of fear and anxiety increased and spilled over into tears of anguish as he lay on the hospital gurney, waiting to be transported upstairs to his room. I cautioned him to not cry as it could provoke further injury. My words (signs) to him went unheeded. I bent over our young son and prayed for God to come and give him His peace. Within seconds Kent fell into a deep sleep. About 30 minutes later, he was still asleep when a nurse came to transport him upstairs. He woke up in the elevator and it was evident that all the fear and anxiety had dissipated.

We sat and visited with Kent in his dark room (he had to lift the patch on his good eye to see our signs.) After a dinner of McDonald's hamburger and chips, his sister and dad decided to go home. It was 10 p.m. and I had decided to stay a little longer to get Kent settled for the night. I got up into the cot with him and tucked him in. I cautioned Kent not to turn over onto his right side, explaining that the doctor had said that more pressure on the eye could predispose a secondary hemorrhage, which in turn would result in retina detachment and ultimately the loss of sight in his right eye.

I was unsure if I should stay all night to ensure Kent would not turn over, but while trying to decide, I asked the Lord about it. His answer was as clear as if He were in the room with me, as indeed He was. The words from Psalm

27:1 "Unless the Lord, keep the city, the watchmen awake but in vain." The Lord was saying that if God did not protect Kent, there was nothing I could do to change it. I decided to go home and rest, committing Kent to God's keeping, and I believe that He sent His angels to take care of him.

This story has a happy ending. Kent was released after a four-day hospital stay, and his eye was fine. Our doctor told me that he was a very fortunate boy not to have lost his eye. He said that somebody was looking after him.

God is faithful in our time of trouble. "When they call on me, I will answer. I will be with them in trouble. I will rescue them and honor them." Psalm 91:15. This is truly a tribute to God's faithfulness!

A Loving Mother and Daughter

In Christ Jesus

Shirley W.

Miracle 35

Our God is a God of Miracles.

There are very few Christians that would disagree with that statement. I have been the recipient of several of those miracles: let me tell you about just one.

It was 1986 and we were living about 100 miles from Calgary. My daughter and I had heard there was to be a "spirit filled" conference in Calgary with Father Robert DeGrandis as the facilitator. We were very excited and registered for the whole thing.

It was decided to take my granddaughter along. She was twelve years old at the time. I remember during the Saturday session that Father Bob asked how many in the group wanted to receive the gift of tongues. There were so many people that put their hands up that he decided to have a workshop right there and then. He had the people line up and come to him one at a time. As he prayed for each individual he asked the rest of the congregation to pray as well. The result was wonderful! We saw each person return to their seat speaking in a different language.

All weekend I had been praying, asking God to heal me. I had a frozen shoulder and for those of you who don't know what they are: it is this. Every movement just freezes up and you have no mobility or range of motion in your shoulder! At that time I had been going to therapy at the hospital for nine months with only a slight improvement in my condition. I could just raise my hand up about waist high.

We were just finishing Mass and worshiping God in the last hymn and I remember thinking "Well I guess this isn't the right time for my healing", being the impatient person I am I was surprised at how accepting I was of that fact. As I went to lift my hands up in praise, the tears started to pour down my face and my hands went up and up and up: until they were away above my head!

God is ALWAYS full of surprises!!! Although my shoulder aches at times, I have never had any restriction in my movements from that time to now, which is twenty three years later!

I love you Jesus! PRAISE and THANKSBE TO GOD!!

You are my Joy, Lord,

Margaret

Miracles 36

What is a Miracle?

According to the Webster Dictionary, a miracle is "a "Supernatural" event regarded as due to a divine action".

For me, Miracles (divine actions) are all around us, happening every minute, everywhere. The real miracle occurs when we are granted the Grace to recognize one in our own life.

This is one of those times.

My husband and I were expecting our first child. As most people would, we expected and prayed for a happy, healthy child and prepared the usual things like the nursery, new little clothes, etc. We did not expect the doctor to come to us a few days after the birth of our beautiful baby boy and say, "Don't worry, but we think there is something wrong with your son and we will be doing some tests". That's when I really started praying!

As the weeks went on and the medical tests continued – I prayed for a miracle. I was watching our son getting weaker. I prayed harder. When I closed my eyes to pray I could see this candle with its flame burning fitfully as if in a strong wind. More time passed with no answers from the doctors. Our son was in more distress. I prayed more and the candle flickered as if in great distress from the wind.

Six weeks after the birth of our son, with no answers as to why, our son died.

I was angry with God. He didn't answer our prayers. I didn't want to pray because I knew the flame on the candle would be gone – extinguished!

This doesn't sound like a miracle, but here it is.

Eventually, I just knew I had to return to praying, even if I had to face the extinguished flame of my son's life.

As I prayed that first night of prayer: I closed my eyes and there was the candle burning brightly and peacefully! In that moment I knew that God is the eternal caregiver of my son, myself and of us all.

Anonymous

But known to God

Miracle 37

I am Grateful!

The following are events that happened in my life, which I consider miracles.

First of all, I think back to the time I was a small boy about 5 years old. My three sisters, and I, were in an old ModelA car, which our dad had left running while he was conversing with a nearby farmer.

It was cold out and that's why our dad had left the car running. I believe there was a hole in the floor boards of the vehicle, which allowed the exhaust to enter the car. The next thing you know my sister, Phyllis and I are laying on the floor of the car passed out.

The other two older sisters were in the front seat of the car and they were not yet affected by the carbon dioxide. Luckily they noticed that Phyllis and I were in grave trouble, so they hollered at our dad, who was standing just a few yards away from the vehicle.

Dad and my Uncle Abe came running over, saw my sister and I lying on the floor, then grabbed us and took us out into the fresh air outside. After several minutes of doing what they could to revive us, we both started breathing again. WOW! What a near miss!

Thank my Heavenly Father, for the quick actions of all who participated in our survival.

When I was around 13-14 years old, I went for a rabbit hunt with two of my cousins, with whom I was spending some time with at their farm. I remember it was a cold, winter, day and of course we were on foot.

We had walked a few miles searching for rabbits to shoot with our 22's. As I was not dressed warm enough for the occasion, I soon began to shiver from the cold. I felt that I could not carry on any further, so I told my two cousins to go on ahead without me and so, off they went.

While I was waiting for them to return, I saw a rabbit hopping close by. I tried to pull the trigger of the 22 rifle that I was carrying but at this point my fingers were frozen and I couldn't. A few more minute's passed and my cousins returned to my location.

At this point, I was starting to feel delirious and felt like I would go to sleep. My cousins realized my condition wasn't good, so they decided to assist me in walking to a nearby Country Church, which was about ½ mile from where we were at. Once we got there, my cousins took me into the Church, which was not locked. Then they started a fire in the wood furnace and I was able to warm up enough to begin the two mile trek backto their farm.

The miracle here was, that little forgotten, unlocked Church on the prairie! Again, thank you Jesus, for without heat that cold day in winter, I would have frozen to death! Again my life was in Your Hands and You protectedme!

I believe it was in the year of 2005 in July. My wife and I were in Brandon Manitoba to visit her parents, as we usually go there at least once a year to see them. They are getting on in age and are unable to do some of the heavy work they used to do.

One night we were sitting at the dining room table having supper, whena discussion began about painting the exterior of my wife's mom and dad's house. As my wife's mom and dad often differ on their opinions, a very heated discussion ensued as to when and who would be hired to paint the house. I could see that this discussion was going nowhere, as the voice decibel levels were raising and that the finger pointing was continually revolving around the table.

Suddenly a thought came to me. I said, "Why don't we all join hands and pray for God's mercy and help in this matter." And so all agreed and we prayed for God's help together. After our prayer, all of us seemed relieved and we all went about cleaning up the dishes and such.

The next morning my wife and I were preparing to leave to go back to Redcliff, our home town. We said our goodbyes and away we went. That evening after having arrived back in Redcliff, we got a phone call from my wife's parents. They told us that someone had dropped off a business flyer in their mail box, advertising their business of house painting. They then called the painter and arranged for a meeting and an estimate. Low and behold, they hired the individual and house was painted shortly afterwards.

The year 2008 in July, the Reimer family on my dad's side had scheduled a family reunion. The reunion would take place at Big Stone Regional Park at a lake called "Blood Indian."

As my wife was in Manitoba to see her parents, I was alone in my truck, pulling our trailer out to the campsite at Big Stone. As I was approaching the campsite, I noticed from a distance, a large ominous looking cloud to the northwest of the lake area. To me it looked as though it could produce a very high wind storm or possibly even a tornado. As I had prayed for an excellent reunion and very good weather for mostof the previous year, a thought came to me that a menacing storm now could destroy all our plans for a well desired family reunion.

Again, I quickly turned to the sourceof all my need, The Lord our God, Jesus. I prayed that He would do something about the huge mass of ominous clouds heading for that little lake where we heading. Sure enough, the clouds driftedoff to the northeast and posed only a small amount of discomfort for all of us that had arrived that evening. What had looked crushing turned out to be just a small amount of rain with very little wind. Praise God in Heaven for this Miracle!

My Joy is in the Lord!
Thank you, Jesus
For your Presence
Ernie

Miracle 38

Jesus is Ever Present

I thought I would share a neat coincidence or possible "Miracle" that I came across.

A few years ago my wife and I were watching "The Passion" of the Christ. (Mel Gibson) During the movie one of our children woke up and my wife wentto check on her. I paused the movie andwas waiting patiently. It was about 5 minutes of waiting when I noticed a faceof Jesus appear on the right hand of the screen. I showed it to my wife when she returned and it is really quite amazing. The time on the DVD recording is (1hr: 34min: 29sec.) Jesus is nearing the topof Calvary and is falling to the right. The face appears amongst His clothing. Lots of people that I have shown this to, agree it is quite astonishing. Other people don't see it, or see a lions head. It is hard to see. To find it, again, I paused, the film at the above time and then frame by frame, the picture becomes a little clearer. Jesus' chin is His eye, and His left arm makes the nose and chin. It is a profile. The odds of pausing the film at the exact moment, is alone, amazing. If you have the film, check it out and see for yourself this possible "Miracle."

Thank you, Jesus, for being Ever Present!

Darren and Vicki

Followers of Christ

Miracle 39

Miracle to Blessing

What did I do to deserve this? What had happened in my life to bring me to this point? Why have I been so blessed? How could I ever give back what I had received? Did I do something right somewhere-sometime? Maybe God gave me this just because... These are only a few questions I now face everyday as I look upon my biggest blessing and my true miracle – my daughter, Andree.

Anyone who knew me growing upin Coalhurst, Alberta would know that I was very unpopular, an introverted loner, who tried hard to be accepted, but was ostracized and bullied, especially during my junior high and senior high school years.

I had come from a good family. My parents were both strong faith- filled, practicing Catholics, but as the oldestof four, I was weak when it came to the ways of the world. Often I prayed for the people who were hurting me the most at school. I kept remembering Jesus on the cross, saying, "Forgive them, Lord, they know not what they do." This, for many years, was my prayer and my strength.

The year is 1993. I am pregnant because of a bad choice: a single mother at the age of twenty-nine years. My due date is set for April 22nd, 1993. I am pretty well on my own. January 4th of 1993 finds me in the hospital with complications due to emotional stress as well as other physical problems. On January 7th, my situation deteriorates. I develop a blood infection and my water breaks. I must have this baby and soon, if we are both going to live.

I am sent to Calgary Foothills Hospital to have my child. I am scared. I really do not want to go there: I am sure that I will only be a "number" in such a large institution. Why am I important? Who will care for my baby and me? Who will save my baby? There is no one there with me during most of this time. I feel truly alone with my child and very uncertain.

In the Delivery Suite, the first nurse I meet informs me that I must get used to the idea of losing this child, and that I will not leave the hospital with a baby. I am flabbergasted! This event simply affirms my earlier fear of being insignificant. I know instantaneously, with all the faith that I possess, that God is totally in control of this situation: and that, NO, this nurse did not know what she was talking about!

I know that the child in my womb was alive and ready for life. I know to baptize the infant in my womb and to give her up to the Lord, no matter what. Love, prayer and hope surround the baby. I picture the infant being held by angels and whisper to her that all will be as God wills.

Because I was only twenty-five weeks along in my pregnancy, I had not taken all the necessary pre-natal education. Such considerations I left in the Lord's hands. The Holy Spirit guided me to decide on an epidural: I knew nothing about such things. The doctors (and there were many in this teaching hospital) informed me of all the possibilities and percentage – including deformity, deafness, blindness, lung damage liver and intestinal problems, cerebral palsy, mental retardation, heart problems, and the list went on. I was told that she had a 5% chance of being born normal.

I knew, again by faith that Our Lord was completely in control and that no matter what the outcome was, I was to accept His will. I knew by faith that we were going to be O.K.

Andree Lilianne Lemire, born on January 8th, 1993 (at twenty-five weeks gestation) at 3:01 A.M., weighing 930 grams (2lbs., ¾ oz.) and 36 cm (14 ½ inches) long. The size of her hand was as small as my thumbnail, and her skin was transparent because she had no pigment yet. She made no sound until she was 3 months old. This was and is my "little miracle". As tiny as she was, she was a HUGE miracle!

Twenty-four hours after her birth, I developed blood clots in both legs in three areas. I was kept in hospital for 3 weeks and Andree stayed for four weeks. At the time, the nursing staff was more concerned about my life than hers, even going so far as to share my situation with their husbands and praying for my baby and for me.

I did not have the opportunity to hold my daughter until ten days after her birth. In the hospital, she went down to 700 grams (approximately 1 ½ lbs.). After four weeks, she was moved to the NICU at the Lethbridge Regional Hospital. She was discharged, one month before her original due date, on home oxygen at 2065 grams (approximately 4 ½ lbs.) 2 ½ months after she was actually born. She was officially baptized in Coalhurst in June, 1993 at six months of age.

After many tests and hospitalizations over the years, hers and mine, my thirteen-year old daughter is now 167 cm (5 feet 6 2/3 inches) and weighs over 65 kg. She is physically fit, regularly participating in Ringette and other activities. She is an Honor student in Grade Eight at St. Francis Junior High School in the French Immersion Program. The only residual effect from her premature birth is a chronic lung disease – due to scarringon her lungs. This condition is controlledquite effectively now with medication.

I am very proud of my daughter, butI know that all the glory is truly our Lord's. Her faith relationship with our Lord is constantly growing, and we both live according to the Christian/Catholic faith. She has been told from a very early age that she, indeed, has been given so much, and she knows that she must lovingly give back.

During my pregnancy, due to hormones and stress, I triggered a hereditary illness, which causes blood clots. I eventually had seven deep vein blood clots in twenty-eight months. At the time of my father's untimely death, I had my last blood clot and was finally diagnosed with Activated Protein C Resistance. I now take a needle every twelve hours and I am challenged daily by physical struggles. I am on permanent disability through AISH, (although I am an educated university and college graduate).

Yet, I consider all of these events, blessings. They are all part of the miracleof my life and my daughter's life. We, together, have learned to budget what we have, to enjoy the simplicity of life,to accept our limitations, but always to strive for what we desire – always with our Lord in mind. We understand that God is in control!

I have, out of necessity, always been the one in Andree's life making all the decisions – always asking the Holy Trinity for guidance. I am very strong now, in faith, in relationships, in my daughter's life, and in the community. This strength would never have happened had these "horrible" things not happened to me.

I like who I have become and I want to always do God's will. He gave me this incredible blessing – our life – and I honor it. Together, my daughter and I will honor it. It isn't always easy, but it is always a blessing. From this wonderful miracle comes our blessing!

By Colette Lemire

(edited version June 13th, 2006)

Know God wants to Bless You!

Miracle 40

You Can't Put God in a Box!

For some people, depending on their personal place of "their own" faith journey, the Holy Trinity is their total portion of their Spiritual walk. For many others, "Mother Mary", is also very active in God's children's daily lives. Yet for many other "praying" or "meditating" Christian Believers, "Saints" and "more" of the "Spiritual world" is revealed, perhaps the Believers own guardian Angel or Angels that are present in their lives. Through growing, Faith and prayer, Jesus Christ, The Holy Spirit and, Yeweh, our Heavenly Father, becomes our best friend and as I have learned on my "Faiths" journey, the closer we come to His Grace, the more He reveals to us, in His Own Time, to His children of "The City of Heaven". Salvation is our second birth, one firstly of Spirit, then Mind and then Soul and with it, our inheritance is unlimited!

Here are three more "Miracle stories", that are also amazing, possibly unbelievable to some, yet true for the story teller and recipient, of God's Holy Miracles! For those of you that don't try to put "Yeweh", Our Heavenly Father,in a box, sit back and enjoy, and for those of you that are not "there" yet, don't give up. Just keep reading His Holy Word, praying, and seeking, for God tells us through His Holy Bible, "It is by My Spirit, Not by Might"! And "If you seek Me, you shall find Me".

Yes, Brother's and Sister's, these are more wonderful Promises to live your life by. These stories are from more of your Christian family, in Faith.

One hot summer day I went to the pasture to check the cattle and windmill. When I got there, I found the windmill broken and the tank dry.

I started to climb the 20 ft. tower with tools in my left hand, jumping from rung to rung, with my right hand. WhenI reached the top my hand was too wideand I missed the little brace that holds the point of the tower together and started to fall back. When something like this happens, your mind races so fast, everything seems to be going in slow motion.

I looked down at the tank that had a cement floor. The rim was a steel wheel from a steamer tractor, eight feet in diameter.

The only thing that went through my mind as I was falling was; If I fall inside the tank my head will hit the rim andI will be dead; or if I fall further outmy back will hit the rim and I will have a broken back and who will look after Lucille and the children?

By this time I was in a horizontal position, so I pushed off with my legs. I floated out and landed on my back, light as a feather, 14 ft. from the tower. I felt absolutely no pain or discomfort. I simply got up, dusted myself off,grabbed the tools and climbed the tower again - this time I went very careful.

Lucille does a lot of spiritual reading and meditating. She read in one of her books that you can ask your spirit guidesor also called your "Guardian Angel" or "Angels" their name. So one evening she asked and waited ... nothing happened. So she turned over and prepared for sleep.

All of a sudden, a loud voice said, "Gloria"! Lucille jumped up, thinking she must have dozed off and was dreaming, when again, a softer voice again said, "Gloria".

Now she talks to "Gloria", or her personal Angel, all of the time. Since she loses or misplaces things a lot, Gloria is very busy, but always there to help. On one occasion, Lucille sawa shirt in a Sears flier that she wanted. When she arrived at the store, the clerk told her they were all sold out. However, something drew her to a rack in the backof the store and there was the shirt shehad wanted and in the exact size and color she wanted!

Our youngest daughter also meditates a lot. One day she and her friend, Charmen, who is a natural healer and sees auras, were having coffee. Charmen looked at Alison and said, "Do you know there is an angel on your right shoulder"? Alison said, "Yes, that's Colett. I talk to her all the time".

Our oldest son, Dave, worked in Golden, B.C. for a few years before moving to Medicine Hat.

A friend of his from Golden died, leaving his house, a cabin in the mountains and a 4-wheel drive jeep to his daughter, who works as a horse chiropractor, at a racing stable in Ireland. She phoned Dave, asking if he would go to Golden and rebuild the cabin so she can rent it out.

He said "yes" and went there in the fall, hoping he could finish before the weather turned cold. However, it rained everyday, slowing him down considerably, as most of the work was outside. The rain changed to snow, to the point, where he could not get up the mountain with his Honda. Regularly, it was a 20 minute drive to the cabin.

She told him to use her jeep, which he did. The second last day he was up there, it snowed all day and he got stuck several times coming down the mountain. He realized, if it snowed some more he would not be able to get back to finish the job the next day.

While doing his meditating and praying that night, he pictured himself driving up the winding trail to the cabin and went to sleep.

Upon waking the next morning he saw it had snowed hard all night and worse still, there was a whiteout. The fog was so thick you could only see a few feet. He realized it was impossible to get to the cabin without help. So he phoned a friend of his, who had a 4 wheel drive tractor with a backhoe and frontend loader.

They agreed to meet at the corner at a certain time. When Dave got there, there was no tractor, so he sat back, closed his eyes and started to meditate and pray.

All of a sudden the jeep started to move on its own. He tried to stop it but it just kept on going up the hill. All he could see on the way up, was the odd black spot push the side window, when an evergreen went by.

The jeep stopped in front of the cabin. When Dave got out he saw the snow was up to the middle of the radiator on the jeep which was about 2 ½ to 3 feet deep. About 2 hrs later the tractor pulled up and his friend asked. "How on earth did you get up this mountain? I got stuck several times and had to dig myself out with the backhoe"!

Again, these "Miracle" happenings are all from the Hand of our Heavenly Father. Though reading and trusting God's Holy Word, our unending prayer and meditation, produce fruit of all flavors. Again, these stories reveal to all that seek His Truth that "Jesus" is in the "Miracle" business and loves you!

Jesus is my Savior

Henry

Miracle 41

The God Given Amazing Photo

Here within these sentences are found incredible, supernatural facts of a picture that was taken and developed eight months after the death of our beloved daughter, only to witness her presence upon the photograph. Let us tell you of our precious, beautiful picture!

Fact #1: Our daughter had died on August 8, 2007.

Fact #2: We bought our first digital camera on February 4, 2008, which also had been our deceased daughter's birthday.

Fact #3: Our cameras first set of digital pictures were developed on November 25, 2008 and the mystery picture was #26 in number order.

So many unusual circumstances surrounded the picture #26. Just previous to April 2008, we took a pictureof an end of March, beginning of April snow storm with this new camera. The mystery picture came just before the winter snow storm picture, #27 and right after a picture of our daughter's most favorite nephew, picture #25. So we figured it must have been taken some time after Valentines Day on February 14th, 2008 and just previous of April 2008. Our Daughter had died about eight months earlier.

First we couldn't believe our eyes and both my husband and I thought, "How could this be"!

This is when we looked into the factsof this unusual photograph.

Fact # 4: This picture is exposed 3 or possibly 4 times. We have been told by numerous people that double exposures are not possible on a digital camera.

Fact # 5: The identification numbers on the back of the picture falls right in number order sequence of all the other pictures.

Fact # 6: This number order of sequence identifies the time line taken.

Fact # 7: One of the exposures was taken upstairs in our house of the kitchen.

Fact # 8: One exposure was taken downstairs of our house in the rumpus room.

Fact # 9: The 3rd exposure was of something like an arm and possible hand in a blessing position beside and slightly above our daughter's shoulder and head. The possible arm and hand looks like the end of a sleeve rolled up at the elbow and sleeve bare, the lower arm and hand.

Fact # 10: We looked back throughout previously developed regular camera pictures and was amazed to find that the clothing that that our Son-In-Law and now deceased Daughter, had the same clothing on, as in a pictures taken on Christmas Day, 2002, which also was taken in our home. However, on Christmas Day, 2002, we have no known pictures with both, husband and wife, in same picture. They each were in separate 4x6 pictures and that was six years previous to the mystery picture!

Fact # 11: The mystery picture was not on digital camera when I deleted and edited pictures before processing and developing disk.

Fact #12: Nowhere on picture disk is there a copy of the mystery picture.

Conclusion: This picture is beyond any logical explanation. We have pondered all angles of mystery picture and have come to the conclusion that: We as Christian Believers in a Mighty Heavenly Father, Jesus Christ, and The Holy Spirit, do believe that we were allowed to receive a non-verbal message from our loving, Jesus Believing daughter, through this "Mystery" picture. With grateful hearts we thank you, Father.

Grateful for God's Presence
R. and C.

Miracle 42

Fractured Innocence

How wonderful to live in the sacred space of Trust: to trust all is well, and trust that ultimately God will provide. Trust that is there from the moment of conception nestled securely in the womb, being formed uninterrupted into a full rational and emotional human being like the remainder of humanity. The miracle of life leaves us bewildered as we contemplate this gift of life, how fragile it remains and what care and love this human being demands for this proper development into maturity.

How wonderful this security of feeling love, living in a deep faith in the sacred space of home and feeling the security of God.

But one day, in one early summer of childhood, what would invade this sacred space was the element of a perverse evil, a force so great as to fracture the temple of God, that of a child.

I was that child, living out the newness of summer not having a care and once again trusting that all would continue well.

Approached by a stranger, and enticed by suggestions of material goods if I but went with him. I trusted and was led into a deep forest, where he had hid a gun under a bush. He retrieved it as we walked along. Panic and fears set in!! What do I do now?! I resigned myself for fear of my life, which I knew would be threatened. I realized I was in a trap, caught in a web and a victim at best!

We walked for some distance in this deep forest and came to a clearing next to a large bolder. A sudden stop and he ordered me to disrobe. I realized I was in trouble as he put the gun to the temples of my head. I had to obey. The greatest violator of the sanctity of human life began; an ordeal that lasted for a few hours. I was being raped!

Later on in a given moment, I saw an opportunity to escape. I ran! He pursued me. As I ran, I stumbled over a large branch. He caught up with me and dragged me along to the clearing uttering death threats that now he would kill me.

At that moment, I lost any will to live. Who was I, a 9 year old boy to overcome a full grown male? I became like rag doll, all strength drained out of me. More rape and torture! Where was my God in all this? I cried out. No answer. I looked up in the sky and at a distance. I saw what I believed was an image of our Lady, the Blessed Virgin Mary! Was it an illusion in a desperate moment of panic? I think not, for an interior voice spoke to me, "I will deliver you. Trust in me".

How could a young boy think of using a reverse psychology with this irrational creature?

I was able to convince him, that if he let me go, I would promise to return with pictures of my sisters. I spoke of how beautiful they were. He became terribly excited and finally after much pleading, he decided to let me go. "Don't tell the police or else the next time I will kill you!"

Upon my release after 4 hours of rape and torture, I'll never forget the tremendous feeling of liberation I felt. Our Lady had led me to freedom. As I walked away, the anxiety was so intense. I finally arrived home. Mother phoned the police. I gave my report, followed by, the next day, being at a police line – up to identify the rapist. This was an eerie experience for a boy, as it wouldbe for any one.

Through this brush with death, Devine providence brought me to safety.

The ongoing saga of my life did not stop here. I lived many turbulent years of adolescence, spent in much soul searching, isolated due to lack of Trust and suspicions.

My father, whom I so longed to know, slighted me, through no fault of his own. I had 6 siblings and felt distanced from them. I felt truly "alone". Reading the

Bishop's Sheen, "Passion of Christ", gave me consolation. I could truly relate to the passion of our Lord, His experience of abandonment.

When I was 19 years old, my father died and was followed by my mother's death a few years later. My parent's were gone. I grieved with such intensity. "My God, my God, why have you abandoned me?" was my cry, as Jesus had cried 2,000 years before. Nothing could console this interior agony. The pain became intolerable, to the point of despair. Hanging by a mere thread, I was prepared to surrender in death, to God. Is this what I was created for? A futile life of emptiness is what I had. I like Job, experienced the loss of all! Faith and hope was all that remained.

On my knees, I cried out in despair, "My God, if you are there, answer me!" I cried, "Dear God, dispel this fear, this coldness and chaos". Finally, once again, fully on my knees, I felt His hand on my shoulder. I was being delivered! It was a literal touch of God! He Saved me a 2nd time from an untimely death!

These were "Graced" moments. I was led to the Sacraments where I grew in God's Mercy and Grace. The years passed have continued healing and today I have been a priest for 25 wonderful years. In a few months, I will celebrate my Jubilie.

I praise and worship the "Mercy of God", for He Saved me from an eternal death. How Merciful is our God!

Reborn and Loved Forever

Miracle 43

God say's "Don't Be Depressed"!

Early in the month of May 2006, I was dealing with a bout of "Poor me" pity pot attitude and emotions. My husband and I have never had a lot of money from our careers and working positions. Emotionally, I guess you could say I was "Down in the dumps". Now in reality, my husband and I, own a small but lovely home, we had and have a wonderful close family body of loving children. We never went hungry and we always have had decent clothes on our backsides.

Now early in the month of May, with my "pity-pot- dull-drums" attitude, I dragged myself around the house. Finally, my loving husband of sixteen year's, could stand it no longer!

As I was sulking in the bath tub, my wonderful, Christian husband walked in and started to "matter-of-factly" ask me questions.

Do you have a car?!

I looked up and replied, "Yes".

Can you drive a car?!

Again, I replied, "Yes".

Can you walk?!

Sheepishly I acknowledged again, "Yes".

Then my sweet husband said, "Can your Mom do any of that"?!

Immediately, I felt very ashamed of myself, because my mother, who at the time was 74 years old, whom for most of her life had never had any of the above, was a woman that never complained. My dear Mother was wheelchair bound for more than half of her 76 years with no "privilege" to walk let alone to drive or own a car.

With this window of humbling reality rearing in my face, I knew I had no good reason to be sad or depressed about money. I could walk, run, drive, work, play and share my life with the man of my dreams. How disappointed I was now, in my "poor me" attitude!

My husband's honest reality check balanced me emotionally for about a week or two, and then I slumped back into my little world of "financial" depression. It was like an uncontrollable magnet and I just couldn't help myself.

Weeks after my husbands raw truth soaked my emotions, I found myself laid on the living-room couch, motionless and heavy with plaguing depression. Before I had laid down, I had turned on the television set and tuned onto "channel 4", my favorite channel, that being the Miracle Channel.

Too gloomy to notice "what program" was being televised, I plunked my sorry self, heavily onto the receiving couch, laid down, closed my eyes and just wallowed in a sleep depressed condition.

I don't know exactly how long I had laid there in my toxic condition, but low and behold what happened next was so amazing, it's almost impossible to believe!

On the couch, sound asleep because of depression, I all of a sudden heard someone, a man's strong voice, yelling my name! Like I said, I was in quite a deep sleep, but the man just kept on yelling my name! Strongly and loudly I heard, "Lana, Lana!! "Lana, wake up!! Get off of that couch!! You are depressed but you DON'T have to be!! God loves you!! God is with you right now!! He will never leave you or forsake you!! Trust Him!! Get up, Lana!! Do NOT be Afraid!!"

Well like you, I couldn't believe my ears or then next, my eyes! I opened my eyes, hearing the force of the man's voice and then seeing the man look at me through the television set. God, through the Miracle Channel, was somehow calling out to me through this Pastor. First this man had to wake me up from a depressed sleep and then relay the wonderful message from our Holy Trinity!

Immediately, I sat up! Then quickly while watching and listening to the man of God, I stood up, literally shaking off all the black depression that was nestled in my mind and body! I looked around seeing no one else in our house, but knew without any doubt, that Jesus and the Holy Spirit, was right beside me!!

One thing I learned beyond any doubt is: God's love and presence for and with us, reaches into every cornerof our lives, whether we are sleeping, walking, talking, alone or in crowds!! Jesus is "Always" present!! Even if I don't "feel" His Presence, He is only a "thought" away! We are Never alone!

As you can image, with the Holy Spirit using a "mere man" on the Christian Channel to pierce the ugly depression and remove it from my being, is one more, huge "Miracle" that I am forever grateful for! Since that Holy Spirit altering moment, I am overjoyed to say that "depression" is not within my human spirit anymore! That bout of depression was over four years ago and since that experience, with my whole being I "Do" trust my Heavenly Father, Jesus, His Son and His Amazing Holy Spirit!!

Thank you, Father, King of Kings, Best Friend and Physician!! Every time you "Save" me, my faith grows and I love you more. Great is your Glory!

May all hearts open to Jesus' Love

Lana

Miracle 44

Mom's Answered Prayers

When I was younger, my family and I lived on 7th Street N.W. in Medicine Hat. My Mom was always nervous watching my sister Michele and I walk to school and have to cross the corner of 7th Street N.W. and Bassett Crescent N.W. The winter months were particularly nerve-racking for Mom. The roads could be like skating rinks. Mom would watch us cross that street and walk around the corner, until she couldn't see us anymore. My Mom remembers praying that God would keep us safe.

One wintry day of my last year at St. Michael's Elementary School, I crossed 7th Street and walked along Bassett heading towards Terrill Rd. where I would turn left. The roads were very icy that day. A car turned right from Terrill Road onto Bassett and suddenly it hit some ice. It started to do a 180 and the car started coming towards me. I then felt a gentle shove on both of my shoulders and I fell back in the snow. The front passenger side wheel of the car came up on the sidewalk exactly where I shoved. The driver side of the car door opened and a man jumped out because he thought he had hit me. He asked if I was okay and I told him I was fine. He then went over to his car and asked his granddaughter, who was in the passenger seat, if she was okay. She was frightened and upset. He then came over to me again and asked a second time if I was alright. I then realized that where I had fallen into the snow was so far up on the lawn that there was no way I could have just fallen over with a "gentle shove".

I got up and walked to the sidewalk and looked back at my footprints in the snow. It was then that I realized it was my guardian angel that protected me!

My Mom's prayers were answered!

Submitted by Colleen Carr

Miracle 45

Our Guardian Angels

My sister, Colleen and I both worked at Future Shop in Medicine Hat. We were driving home after work. I was driving and Colleen was in the passenger seat. We were listening to music quite loudly. Just as we were approaching the top of the Allowance Avenue Overpass (when it was just a single lane), Colleen told me to move over to the right! "What?" I asked. "Move over to the right more", she replied. I did, without questioning her. We were quite close to the cementrailing of the bridge, when all of a sudden a Police car came speeding upthe overpass directly towards us in OURlane with his lights flashing and sirenson.

He saw us and swerved over, fast, to the other lane and a second police car followed him. My sister and I were in shock! We drove to the bottom of the overpass and pulled over. I shut off the music. We were shaking. I asked Colleen, "What made you say move over"? and she said, "I don't know, it just came outof my mouth".

We knew that if we hadn't moved over, we would have gotten into a head-on collision with the police car. We didn't hear the sirens because the music wasso loud. We both said together, "That was our guardian angels, protecting us"!

Submitted by Michele (Carr) Bottomley

Miracle 46

The Nightmare Intersection

One of my worst nightmares about driving in the winter is getting stranded in the middle of an intersection, in a vehicle, by my-self. This nightmare was about to come true!

One cold wintry day in Medicine Hat, I was driving my husband's old pickup truck to work. I was coming down Altawana Drive from Crescent Heights and stopped at the red light at the bottom of the hill at Parkview Drive N.E. The light turned green and I started to go. Unfortunately, I only got about six feet and the truck stopped... right in the middle of the intersection. I tried turning the key and pumping the gas pedal to no avail. I knew I had flooded the engine. It was such a busy intersection with traffic headed in all directions!

I put my head down on top of the steering wheel and prayed, "Please, help me Lord". Just at that moment there was a knock at my window. I opened the window. A wonderful gentleman informed me that he was directly behind me with his truck, and, if I didn't mind, he could push my vehicle across Altawana Bridge and into the parking lot on the other side. All I felt was relief! His truck pushed my truck along the bridge and into the parking lot on the other side.

He came to the window and said, "Start the truck", and I said, "It's not going to start". He said again, "Start your truck". Something about the way he said it, I just knew it was going to work.

I started the truck. I turned and thanked him immensely! He smiled and turned away. A thought just came to meat that moment and I knew he was my guardian angel sent to me in answer to my prayer!

I quickly looked in my rear view mirror, but he and his truck were not there. I turned around to look for him, but I knew I wouldn't see him.

Submitted by Trish Carr

Miracle 47

My Guardian Angel on Duty!

Picture this near my office... a four-way intersection – there are no stop signs or yield signs.

My story begins like this...

As I approached the intersection to turn left, a truck was proceeding to drive THROUGH the intersection. I could see a crash happening; but I felt, a tug, like my vehicle was, very slowly, moving back or away. When our vehicles stopped, they were within INCHES from each other, next to the curb.

The male in the truck backed up and proceeded through the intersection. I proceeded ahead, parked the car and went into the office – all shook up! I looked through the office window and the fellow had stopped, got out of his truck and walked toward the intersection. He shook his head and looked very confused. In reality this should have been an accident!

How did we both escape this crash? It's simple – my guardian angel protected me that day!

Note: This happened about 10 years ago and it seems like yesterday! So clear! So vivid!

Believer and Child of God

DF

Miracle 48

Once Terminal, Now Cancer Free

Praise The Living God

Winter was approaching and every thing went from normal to abnormal in my dear friends life. My friend of 30 some years has always marched to her own drummer and is considered quite independent and in control. However, her life of self-control was soon to take a path of sickness, worry and doubt. She was all of a sudden not in control of her life. Her very existence was soon to be at stake. Most of the time, we as independent humans, don't think of death and dying, but when the C word strikes, that being Cancer, we have no choice but to think of death.

Now let's go back to my dear friend, Emily. As the month of November 2008 was unfolding, Emily found that she was very nauseated. She had been only drinking water with lemon juice for quite some time and now it seemed she was unable to eat much food either.

After many urgent visits to the emergency at the hospital and yes many emergency visits to her doctor, she was informed that they thought she may have Cancer of the stomach.

Emily was then tested b y a large medical piece of equipment in Calgary that revealed she had a 15 cm Cancerous tumor in her stomach. She had a dark cloud shadow of something negative over her liver and her main stomach artery was being strangled.

She was slated, as quickly as possible, for surgery in the Medicine Hat Hospital. Her operation date was at the end of December 2008. Hopefully, we thought that the doctors could remove the tumor surgically.

The month of December passed slowly and finally the hospital date came.

Emily made it through this terrible body invasion but shortly after the operation, we learned that after the doctors opened her stomach, she very quickly had to be sewn up!

Since the tumor was 15 cm long and her main artery was strangling the very flow of blood life circulation to her body, the doctors had to sew her up very soon after opening her or she would have bled to death.

Her operation took many long weeks of resting to overcome. The prognosis of this 50 year young woman really didn't look very promising.

About a month passed after the surgery and the doctors scheduled another, "Pet", scan in Calgary. This time they had more pictures of the 15 cm tumor, a black cloud over the liver and also the strangling Cancer around the main stomach artery.

Emily was indeed in a very serious point in her young life. She came back to Medicine Hat from Calgary with the horrible news that she may only have a year or so left here on Earth. That meant perhaps December 9f 2009, we might be going to her funeral! God Forbid!

Now, Emily has many dear friends and upon hearing the deathly news, one of her life long friends of over 30 years, took it upon herself to ask Jesus to heal Emily. Her friend phoned the Miracle Channel, Benny Hinn Ministries, One Hundred Huntley Street, St. Pauls Luthern Church in Medicine Hat and also Christ the King, Pentecostle Church of Medicine Hat as well.

Prayer for Emily was sent up to God, across two countries. Emily's friend informed Emily that hundreds of Born Again Believers were lifting her up to God and were praying and believing for Jesus to totally heal Emily's Cancerous body.

In January 2009, right after Emily was told her life's logical destiny by her surgeon, she consented to taking Kemo Theraphy at our local hospital. Her body was slowly healing from her invasive surgery in December 2008 and now was confronted with, again, the unknown medication, Kemo.

In years earlier, Emily's only sister died at a young age of "Ovarian" Cancer and Emily remembers how violently sick, her sister got, firstly from the Cancer and also from the Kemo.

Please Jesus, intervene in Emily's possible death sentence.

The Kemo sessions where scheduled for once every 3 weeks. Emily's hair fell out. By the Grace of God, she was only a bit nauseated after her Kemo sessions. Many times her largest discomfort was that of fatigue. She stayed mostly in her home, rested, took care of her family as she was able and at the same time, hundreds of Believers kept lifting her up to God, behind her war zone.

A few months passed and Emily patiently went through her daily, weekly schedule. Finally it was time for a Doctors report on her medical situation. Emily went to Calgary and had another "Pet" scan. Two weeks later, Emily was given her results.

Praise God! Good news! The black shadow over her live r was gone! The tumor had shrunk to about 7 cm. The artery was still being strangled.

Praise Jesus, the Cancer was being defeated! The doctors then told her that she may have 2 to 3 years left to live.

Again, Praise God, the Almighty Father was in the process of answering prayers to heal Emily.

The Kemo appointments just kept coming. Life consisted of hospital visits, staying home, resting, taking care of her grandchildren and now hoping for a second chance of life.

July of 2009 came and it was time again for yet another Calgary "Pet" scan. And again, Emily had two more weeks to wait for the medical test outcome.

Finally, the morning of August 10, 2009, Emily went to receive her prognosis of life. This was only 8 months after her surgery and the prognosis of having about a year left to live.

In the company of her family Doctor the medical report was read to Emily, actually two times, because she couldn't believe the report the first time. Officially Emily was told professionally that she is Cancer Free! There is absolutely no tumor, no black shadow over her liver and her stomach main artery is free from being strangled!

Praise the Lord! Jesus heals His Children and answers our prayers!

With overflowing joy this woman, with many friends, broke down and cried many tears of relief.

Later I asked Emily what the Doctor said about this outcome and she told me that her Doctor stated: "By the Kemo treatment and the Grace of God, she is now Cancer Free and well"!

May Emily know in her heart and mind that Jesus, Father God and The Holy Spirit, Loves her with All His Heart and will never leave her or forsake her. His Holy Word proclaims that promise and I accept it, in Jesus' Name.

Emily's   anonymous   friend,

Who loves her also, In Jesus Name

Miracle 49

Your Faith Does Not Rest in The Wisdom of Men but the Power of God

---

I Cor. 2:5

June 5, my mother passed away. Her funeral was held on June 9th. On the next Sunday, June 12, we had gone to Strathmore area where our sons lived. My husband, Clarence, took the dogs for a walk. Afterwards, Clarence went for a shower and seemed to take a long time finishing. After quite a while of waiting for him to return to the family, we became puzzled as to what was taking him so long to shower? The bathroom door was locked and dad was not anywhere to be found so we pried the lock open and there we found Clarence unconscious on the bathroom floor.

Immediately, Dianne, our daughter, called 911 and within 5 minutes the EMC was at our front door. I, Betty, Clarence's wife, rode with the emergency crew to the hospital and it was in the back of the Emergency Van that God spoke to me. God gave me a scripture that, during the whole ordeal, I clung to as referringto Clarence's very "Breath of Life". The scripture revealed was," Your faith does not rest in the wisdom of men, but the power of God". I Cor. 2:5.

On arrival of the Calgary Foothills Hospital, the Doctors and Nurses took over with test after test. Doctors said Clarence didn't look like he had had a heart attack or stroke, but something was terribly wrong. He was extremely confused!

He was taken to have a Cat Scan and again had a seizure and it was then seen that Clarence had an aneurysm on the right side of his brain. He was the admitted to the Intensive Care Unit to stabilize his condition.

Monday, June 13 the doctors decided that Clarence had 2 more aneurysms and an operation was ordered for himas soon as possible. At 4:00 p.m. the nurse and Doctor arrived at the ICU to take Clarence to the O.R. and later at 10:00 p.m., Clarence was again brought back to the ICU room.

Day 3, June 14, Clarence had a bit of an improved day. He was able to move slightly his fingers and toes on command. However, his left side was a lot slower responding. At one point he opened his eyes, recognized Michelle, our daughter and a tear came to his eye.

More problems seemed to present themselves, such as increased blood pressure and swelling in the "clipped" area of one of the aneurysms. Another Cat Scan was then taken.

Day 5, June 16, Doctors didn't like Clarence's set back. Clarence was very sleepy and there was no movement with his left hand and his eyes wouldn't open either.

That night I was feeling very worried of what was happening to my husband, so in despair and truth I approached Jesus in prayer. "Please, God, I don't know what is happening! Please show some sign of recovery in my Clarence's health"! I cried out to my Heavenly Father when I was so over whelmed with grief and sorrow and realized again, Clarence's medical outcome was indeed in God's hands. Again I remembered the scripture in the ambulance that the Holy Spirit had given me the day of our ride to the hospital. Again I clung onto that precious word from God!

The next day, Praise God, there were a couple of much needed signs of delivery. Clarence's temperature was running high, so the doctors lowered it and then his blood pressure went up. The nurse asked Clarence to raise his hand and by the grace of God, Clarence answered, "Which one"? With his temperature down, Clarence then said to me, "I cold" and then he took my hand and raised it up while squeezing it tightly!

Day 7, June 18, the day was looking up with some good news! My sweet husband was responding more often. He was moving his legs more often. The doctors asked Clarence who I was. He looked at me and his response to thatfor quite some time was, "Mrs. T Bone". Asked again, what was his favorite song, he replied, "Jingle Bells, Coco Shells".

Well Michelle, our daughter was filled with laughter with such incredible responses. We believe now that by God's Love and Grace, we were given a lighter side of the moment and situation.

On this 7th day, Clarence was also able to lift his left hand and put it down gently again. As we watched in anticipation of his wellness, all of a sudden, the automatic on and off, corner sink, turned on with water flowing outof facet, while no one was even close to it. Water flowed for a minute or so, andthen turned off again. As soon as the water had stopped flowing out, Michelle responded, "God is washing His hands". We again remembered the Holy Scripture God had given us and yes, Jesus the Physician and Counselor was doing what He does best, that being, loving and healing His children's wounds.

Over the next period of time, Clarence really was amusing in his state of repairing. I would ask him questions like, "What are you doing?" and he would respond, "Not much to look at!" Then Michelle would ask him, "What are you trying to do?" and he would answer, "Trying to get out of here!". Statements like, "You make a pretty good looking Chicken!" , "Go to bed Elephant", "Gather it tomorrow", "That walls got to get up!", "Those fish are good for spawning!", and many times my favorite saying was, "I'm happy, happy, happy!" were said and repeated.

The days just kept on unfolding with minor achievements and a few set backs at times, but again we as a family stood on God's promise to us and we thanked him for His presence.

Clarence was monitored closely by the doctors and nurses and their skilled hands were gentle, professional and loving. Through the next year, Clarence's mind cleared, his walking and talking skills returned and my husband of many, many years was declared a walking, talking miracle of God.

At the start of our medical journey on June 12, Clarence was given only 25% of a chance that he would live, let alone function normally in life. It had been said that even if he lived, he would probably have to have 24/7 professional health care in a health care unit.

Now Clarence and I, Betty, live in our home, healthy and normal. Clarence needs no extra care and our lives are once again full with life's activities and adventures.

Praise Jesus, our Almighty God the Father and the precious Holy Spirit that Clarence's health is now fulfilled by God's Holy Word scripture, "Your faith does not rest in the wisdom of men but the power of God" I Cor. 2:5

God has again stood behind his Word and we love Him with all our hearts for His Truth and unending Love!

Our God is an Awesome God!

Clarence and Betty

Miracle 50

Eight Day Medical Miracle

During a routine physical check up, my doctor through blood work found my white blood count way out of order. My white blood cell count was 211 instead of the normal 11 count. I had given the blood sample at 8:00 a.m. Thursday October 2nd, 2009. At 1:45 p.m. the same day, my doctors' receptionist was on the phone, calling first me, at home but I couldn't be reached because I was outside on the roof of our carport fixing the roof.

Immediately after ringing my home and not getting me, the receptionist called my wife, Lana on her cell phone. Lana had just gotten to work at 1:00 p.m. and was upstairs at her employers' home, putting laundry away, when she received the emergency call.

Christa, the receptionist, asked Lana to find me so, both of us, could come to our Doctor's office as soon as possible. Our Doctor's office was scheduled to close at 1:00 p.m. and Lana was aware of that. Lana told Christa, she would try to locate me, find someone else to pick up the children from school for the family she works for and come as soon as possible with me her husband, Neil.

Lana hung up her cell phone and while still up stairs, she heard someone downstairs in the kitchen. Now Lana's bosses never, ever seemed to come home for lunch, especially on Thursdays. Lana got downstairs on the main floor and there standing was one of her bosses, the father of the children Lana looked after.

Lana told her boss the emergency news and within minutes her boss told her to go home to me. He said he would pick up the children from school, not to worry.

Lana was home in fifteen minutes, where I had just received the telephone message from Lana, saying she was on her way home to get me for the doctor's office. I had just got down off of the roof, so I changed my clothes and we headed out.

It was now 2:30 p.m. or so and our Doctor was patiently waiting. Then came the news. Doctor sat us down and proceeded to tell me that my blood count was out of wack. She said I had a form of Leukemia. Which one, she didn't know at this point.

Then our sweet, wonderful Doctor asked us if she could pray for us while we were there. Of course we both said, "Yes, Please do!" My wife, of almost 19 years, is a Born Again Christian and I have all my life believed in the Holy Trinity and together we felt God's Holy Presence as our Doctor prayed. We agreed in unison for Jesus to take over this negative situation in our lives and our Doctor prayed to "Break off generational curses of this illness"!

The diagnosis and prayer complete, we gathered ourselves and the last comment our Doctor said to me was, "Neil, I give you my word that I will do everything in my power to get the ball rolling as fast as possible, to get you as well as possible as quickly as possible!" With that said, we were on our way out. Our Doctor gave me an appointment paper for a Bone Marrow procedure for the following Tuesday, October 6th, which was made only moments before our phone call to us.

Friday, Saturday and part of Sunday we took ourselves to our little house in Eastend, Sask., just to get away. Sunday we arrived home shortly after lunch time. We unpacked and decided to go to church that evening at Holy Family Parish. We were early for church so we went to Walmart to get some groceries first. We didn't see anyone we knew but it was as though God wanted to get our attention. For the three days since the diagnosis, Lana and I had spent almost every moment together in prayer, out loud to Jesus.

As we walked through the express checkout lane, it seemed so obvious to us that Jesus was walking with us when we tried to pay the cashier. We owed about $40.00. Lana gave $20.00 cash and was prepared to pay with debit the other $20.00. However, as the cashier received the cash, the cash register closed and the debt was cleared! The poor lady behind the cash register was totally dumbfounded, couldn't believe what she was witnessing and frantically tried to figure out the problem. Finally she called her supervisor, reopened the till and then after about ten minutes of confusion, we paid our remaining balance. It was as if Jesus was cancelling our debt and He wanted us to know that!

I took the paid for goods out to the truck and Lana went back into the store for a container of milk.

She told me later that when she went through the express check out again, that this time, there was an older, about 58ish year old, heavier set woman, with a modest dress and no coat, standing in front of her. Lana was quite warm with her heavy coat on. After a few minutes in line had passed, Lana seeing that the woman in front her, was coatless, said "Hello", to the woman stranger. Lana commented that a person didn't know what type of coat to wear in this weather.

The stranger and Lana had a short conversation, when all of a sudden the woman said that she was a "Christian". Lana replied that she was a "Christian" also. The woman stranger then responded that she is a "Born Again Christian". Lana then responded that she also is "Born Again Christian". Lana had an immediate feeling of kinship with this total woman stranger.

The woman started talking about biblical prophecy concerning, now a days, happenings. She asked Lana what church she went to and Lana answered, "St. Pat's".

That's when the line started to move forward and Lana and this amazing, foreign accented, woman concluded there chance meeting in Walmart, Medicine Hat. Lana bought the milk, came out to our truck and told me that that was the only person she had talked to all day, besides me. It crossed her mind that like the Bible says, "People can entertain Angels and not know it". After that unusual conversation, it felt to Lana that she may have been talking to God, The Father, Himself or some other Heavenly Being.

Now back in our truck, we took off for Holy Family Parish and enjoyed a beautiful sermon of "Husbands and Wives oneness". We sang and prayed and listened and then went home.

Once our coats and shoes were off, we settled down to watch some TV in our warm living room at home. We turned on the Miracle Channel and there right in front of us was Pastor Haggee, ministering to us on "Asking Jesus into our personal lives and being Saved now and eternally. He was right in the middle of his Salvation message and The Holy Spirit was all around us and on us.

I said the "Sinners" prayer, asked Jesus into my heart, gave Him my heart and asked Jesus to give me a personal purpose for God, The Father, in my life.

I felt Jesus' presence as He washed, with tears of joy, away the black spots of sin from within my heart. He cleansed me of all my resentments, fears and false pride, as I kneeled at the base of The Cross.

Pastor Hagee's, Miracle Channel, program was sent for me to take part in, that October 4th, 2009, evening at 8:00p.m., just for me. Praise God for Jesus, His Son.

My Doctor had scheduled me for Tuesday, October 6, 2009, for a Bone Marrow extraction at the hospital lab. Being very fearful of this procedure, as people had told me many horrible stories of extreme pain and much discomfort, Lana and I prayed and knew that Jesus was with us and prayed that He was in control. However, the closer and closer for this procedure, the more I was fearful. I prayed for the least amount of trauma as possible. I prayed and Lana prayed with me. Again, I asked the Lord to come into my heart and asked for forgiveness all my sins, then again I handed myself over to Jesus, my Lord.

The morning of the medical test, I envisioned Jesus dying on the cross, and thought that if He died that horrible, painful death for me, then I too wouldbe able to endure a little pain in contrast to His great pain of death by dying onthe Cross, taking All man- kinds black, horrible rejection and sin.

Just before the Bone Marrow Doctor came into my room, Lana and I discussed whether or not Lana would stay in the room with me or go out into the waiting room. Lana stated that she felt in her spirit that she would be more useful outside praying for me.

With that decided, the Doctor camein and Lana left.

I was asked to turn onto my right hand side, elevating my left hip. As I was laying on the bed, the doctor started the procedure.

The pain was enormous for about 3 seconds. The medical device was stabbed through my skin, through my hip bone and deep into the bone marrowof my upper thigh. I cringed, closing my eyes tightly. With great pain, I all of a sudden opened my two eyes and therein front of me by the window, was Jesus on the Cross. Instantly on seeing Jesus, the pain ceased. From that moment on, I felt pressure but by the Grace of God's only Son, there was no more pain! For the rest of the procedure, I was consumed of Jesus' presence and very soon, painlessly, the procedure was over.

The Doctor and nurses left the room and Lana was by my side shortly after. When Lana came in I was lying on my back on the bed, resting quietly. Lana asked me how I was feeling and I told her, "Not too bad". I told her what had just happened and that I had seen, "Jesus' thorns" on His Head.

Lana was in awe and told me what she had been doing during my procedure also.

She had ended up in the Hospital's Chapel and there had been in prayer for over ½ an hour. She said she had felt The Holy Spirits Presence. While praying and crying out to Jesus, Father God and The Holy Spirit, The Holy Spirit spoke to her and told her three things. The first word was, "He is your best friend". The second word spoken was, "He is not going to die". And the third word spoken was, "You will be together forever".

Lana told me also, that when I told her that I had seen Jesus on the Cross, she immediately knew Jesus came to take my pain onto the cross. Praise Jesus my Holy Savior!

After Lana and I shared this incredible Miracle with the nurse assigned to me, we gathered our jackets and wenthome.

When we got home, we were the recipients of a Calgary Tom Bakker Hospital phone message. We were instructed to call as quickly as possibleto secure a Doctors appointment. Within moments it was set, I was due to see the specialist on Friday, October 9, 2009 at 9:30 a.m.

Thursday evening, two days later, we arrived at my brothers' and sister-in-laws' home in Calgary to stay the night. The next morning we were at Tom Bakker Hospital by 8:00 a.m. We were at the Hospital from 8:00 to about 4:30 p.m. and during that time we seemed to have a day full of waiting, waiting on a blood test, waiting for the Bone Marrow test, waiting for our appointment, waiting for instructions, just a day of waiting.

When we did see the wonderful young Doctor, we were filled with relief. The Doctor told me and my wife that out of the four types of Leukemia, I was diagnosed with the one that CAN be put into remission. Another huge Miracle! Thank you Jesus!

With great relief and amazement we left the Calgary Hospital and drove home to Medicine Hat.

In eight days, I had been diagnosed with a type of Leukemia, rededicated my life to Christ, had a bone marrow procedure, seen Jesus on the Cross, been given a diagnosis of being able to put my disease into remission and lastly, on the eighth day, been put on medication that is covered by the government. Only God could do something this great!

Jesus literally carried me and my wife for eight days and nights. He is ever present and I Love Him! God IS in the Miracle business!

I would like to publicly thank the Lord, Jesus for carrying me and my wife throughout the eight days, from October 2, 2009 to October 9, 2009, bringing healing to my body and answering my prayers. Praise Be to You, Lord Jesus!

Neil and Lana

Glory to the Almighty Jesus

Who is the Author of Mighty Miracles

Miracle 51

Walking Through Miracles

My husband's father was suffering from Dementia for about three years but after two years of heavy medication the medical staff in the nursing home had decided to change to a different brand of medication. Within two weeks his Dementia seemed to be managed and he actually regained some of his self respect.

December 25th (Christmas Day), we received a phone call from my husband's brother-in-law stating that there was a remarkable improvement in his medical state and we should drive home and see for ourselves. Sure enough he was quite coherent and actually humorous.

January 12th, there was another Tiger Hockey Game and we had Season Tickets but for some reason I was not feeling well and remained at home. At 8:20 p.m. I received a phone call from my sister-in-law requesting to speak to my husband as their father was very ill with blood clots in his lungs and he was requesting to speak with my husband, myself, our daughter and our son. In these years we could not afford these modern cell phones, so I had to call the Arena and requested to have my husband call home immediately! We left almost immediately for our destination but as we were driving along the highway on a clear, crisp, wintery night a large ball of fire headed directly for our vehicle. Before striking the earth, it became very dim and swerved upwards in the sky.

We arrived at the nursing home. My father-in-law was very week but very coherent and received us with teary hugs and kisses. He explained to us that he was very tired and wanted to go home to be at peace with his Lord and Savior, Jesus Christ. He wanted to say his good-byes to our family and to let us know that "He Loved Us!" "I don't want anyone to stay the night with me as I wish to be alone, so you may go and have a rest or a sleep"!

We left the nursing home. At exactly 11:45 p.m. as we were driving to my sister-in-law's and brother-in-law's farm our vehicle suddenly stopped. My husband exclaimed "I filled both tanks with gas before going to the hockey game, so we can't be out of gas"! It was cold andfrosty and we didn't particularly want anyone outside walking for help. Minutes later there was a vehicle approaching and asked if we needed any help. Well certainly we needed assistance, so our15 year old son left with this stranger to go to get help from his uncle and aunt. Minutes later as our brother-in-law and son were approaching our stalled vehicle, my husband tried to start the vehicle one more time and believe it or not it started!

My father-in-law had passed away at 12:15 a.m. and we were at the farm to receive the phone call. Later during our family conversation we questioned who the nice man was who came with help and where did he live? No one knew who he was or where he lived and we could not remember the color, make or year of the vehicle. We also sent our 15 year old son with a complete strangerto get help.

There are greater powers with the world and it is no man or woman! May this testimony of miracles glorify our Ever Present Holy Trinity, Jesus Christ, our Heavenly Father and His Holy Spirit!

In Jesus' Name

Jean

Miracle 52

Another Miracle in the Hat!!

I always thought miracles happened in the Bible or to special people in stressful times and in other places but I found out that wasn't always the case!!

April 18, 2008, I had a very unusual headache and the bottom of my right foot was "fuzzy". I tried to call my neighbor (a fireman) to find out if these were the symptoms of a stroke. N o answer – so did I call 911? No!! I called my brother in Saskatchewan (who knows everything   nearly) and he confirmed my suspicions. He urged me to call 911 and he'd call back to be sure I was in someone's care. I called my daughter and her husband said, "They'd be right out!" When they arrived I started taking orders and they took me "packed bag" and all, to the hospital emergency. The Doctor in emergency recognized my symptoms and booked me for surgery in the Foothills Neurosurgery.

There was a severe snow storm so the air ambulance was grounded. I waited till it could take me to Calgary airport. The ensuring delays caused me to arrive late for the "booked" surgery and the Doctor was gone.

Thankfully a Doctor who had just finished a long surgery took me on for another lengthy surgery. I am forever grateful to him and his fabulous staff!

I have been blessed with truly wonderful family and friends who were "there" for me in body and in prayers – as is my Lord!

Thank you forever!

A BIRS (Brain Injury Recovery Services) technician, after testing me for recovery, confirmed that I am, indeed, a "Walking Miracle"!!

Praise the Lord for all that!!

I am new and fully recovered except for some memory loss, which, I'm told, is "normal" for someone my age and hair color! Thankfully, I am back to piano teaching and enjoying my super family and friends!

E. Hyland

Miracle 53

From the Gutter to Jail

My growing years were spent trying to survive in a home where my father was an abusive alcoholic. He was an army man and he owned 2 rifles and a Colt 45 – Army issued automatic. When he was sober he was a really nice guy, butwhen he was drunk he was dangerous. He tried to kill my mother twice and he broke my oldest brother's ribs several times (the first time my brother was only three years old). My brother told me that when dad was drunk, often he'd take out his guns to clean them or point them around.

One night he opened the basement door and emptied his clip, bullets ricocheting off the walls. Another night he came home and decided he was going to kill the whole family (mom and six kids). He was going to use his 303 to do the dirty deed.

I believe that God intervened! Mom had hidden the 303 shells because he had tried this before. My oldest brother knew where she'd hidden them this time and he took them from there without her knowledge and hid them outside under the front step where no one could find them. It was a good thing too, because my dad had found mom's hiding place, but not the shells and mom was shocked that they weren't there! Can you imagine her relief!?

Life in our house was an overload of terror, torment, anger, and hatred every time my father drank which was almost every night of the week. When he got older he cut it down to every weekend from Friday to Sunday and occasionally during the week. I could hardly wait to get out!

When I left home at the age of fifteen to marry, it only took a short three years until that marriage was over. I was eight months pregnant and had a year and half old baby to raise on my own.

Then I tried a common-law relationship, but in the end my partner had been murdered (shot in the head) because he had knowledge about a drug deal. Again I was left pregnant with a third child. I'd say mentally, by this time, I wasn't doing very good.

After trying several more short relationships over the next few years, I was more than ready to enter into that mysterious world of drugs and alcohol. I hit the drugs hard and fast and got involved in dealing, parties, bars, and with motorcycle club members. I also hit my bottom just as fast!

I was angry, full of fear and resentment topped with rejection and paranoia. I had built an invisible concrete wall around myself for protection and I wouldn't let anyone in and couldn't let myself out: I wanted to – oh, how I wanted to! My feelings were jammed tight in an almost overflowing garbage can inside my inner most being. Even I had a hard time bringing my real feelings forth, I didn't know how to handle them.

About the only time any of my true pain showed was when I drank. Then I had one of those tongues that could slice a person to bits. My mouth was so foul that when my lips parted it was like an offensive sewage stench pouring forth.

Also, I had so much frustration and mixed emotions that when I was angry, quite often, I'd try to put my small fist through brick walls, gyp-rock walls – had to repair a few of those – and mirrors which I usually destroyed. I only took one look at myself and hating what I saw, my fist would shatter my reflection. I'd then walk away feeling even worse because now my hand was cut, bleeding and bruised which would call attention to my great performance.

In some ways I wanted people to know how much I hurt, but in others I was ashamed and embarrassed at my own actions. It wasn't normal and I knew that. I was so full of anger and self-hatred I just needed to release it somehow without hurting anyone else. After six years of this type of living I didn't think it could get much worse. I was destroying my life and ruining my children's lives. They put up with an awful lot from me.

Then unknowingly I married an alcoholic simply because I drank right along with him. We got along great, when we got along. Somewhere in the twenty years of breaking up, moving out and moving back in, we decidedto try the AA program. The drinking was interfering with my husband's job, so we both tried the rehab centre in Regina.

I was the good little wife that was there to support him as he worked out his problem. You see he had the problem not me (or so I thought).

On the third day there, we were allowed outside the center for walk, bad mistake. We discussed our situation and decided this was not for us so we quietly left. Of course we found a bar and had a "few for the road" before we got on the bus for home.

We did more drinking, more fighting and more separating and then tried AA again. This time I tried Regina rehab centre for myself. I stayed the required three weeks and learned how addiction works, and the damage it does to your body and your life. I was feeling good and doing something good for myself. I even made it to the marbling out ceremony. Then I went back home thinking I was cured, but in no time, with the help of my husband, I once again succumbed to the tantalizing taste of a great beer.

I really blew it, and I felt like a huge failure!

The third time I entered rehab, I was going to upgrading school. My counselor saw how much I was struggling, so he helped me get into another rehab centre. I was once again separated from my husband, so I asked my sister to watch my kids while I was away.

It only lasted a little over a week when I received the urgent call from my husband telling me he was now watching the kids, because my sister's boyfriend showed up and demanded that she go home. Her boy boyfriend was out to kill my husband because he assumed that he was having an affair with my sister. So after three nights of no sleep with a loaded 308 under the bed waiting for the freak to show up, he had asked me to come home.

He and a friend of his showed up to get me with an open case of beer in the car. I just couldn't believe this was happening! All I wanted to do was straighten my life out!

On the second day home, I received a phone call from my sister-in-law (who lived 10 miles away in another town) telling me that at that very moment my sister's boyfriend was trashing their place and looking for my husband. She said he had a gun on him and she sounded scared. I heard him in the background and he was yelling and demanding for her to hang up the phone.

Shortly after he left her place she phoned again and said he was on his way to our place and that he was hunting for my husband. We called the police (who were 40 miles away in another town) and they said they would send a car right away. They knew this guy could be dangerous because they had previous dealings with him.

My husband sat outside in the dark with his 308 waiting for the boyfriend to show up, but he never did. We knew he had a police scanner in his truck, so we figured he heard the police were looking for him so he kept on driving.

That was enough to convince us it was time to move. We were not taking any chances of him doubling back when we least expected it. He had killed before and was capable of doing it again.

Three days later we ended up in Medicine Hat, Alberta, where more drinking, bars and fighting happened. However, the geographical move didn't seem to work. This time, however, my husband and I had a long night of drinking and fighting and in the morning he moved out taking most of the furniture with him. After the kids went to school, I sat on an empty shelf smoking a joint feeling totally dejected and looked out the living room window at the clouds and said something like, "God if you're real, I sure need help. I don't know what to do". I was alone, afraid and so very lost. I just didn't know which way to turn and I really didn't expect God to answer.

I went to Welfare and they got me back into upgrading at the College, but even on my own I still couldn't stay straight. In the evenings I'd be stoned or have a few drinks, and then I'd be hung over in school the next day. In the middle of the semester I met an ex drug dealer, and he and his friend helped me with my school work and also talked a lot about Jesus. Every chance they got they evangelized me, and I also met their wives and they too talked about Jesus. They could see my hunger for God, so they asked me to go the Full Gospel Church with them. That was the turning pint in my life.

At the end of the service there was an alter call for anyone who wanted to accept Jesus as their Lord, so I walked up to the front and said the sinner's prayer. I asked for forgiveness for my sins and asked Jesus into my heart. I felt so peaceful when I left the church that night.

A week later I had a deep desire to go to church again. I also noticed I'd been without a drink or any drugs for the whole week. I had absolutely NO desire for them! I even stopped using my favorite F word! I then realized God had performed a supernatural miracle on me! I tried to quit drinking, drugs and swearing on my own, but never could accomplish it even with the helpof AA and the rehab centre. What I really needed all along was God!

I realized too that God had answered my prayer the day I looked out the window smoking that joint. He didn't care that I was stoned. He cared about my heart and my heart had cried out to him that day. Almost a year later He again delivered me from a twenty-one year old smoking habit that was literally killing me!

Almost three years later I found and joined the 12 Step Serenity Recovery Program (Bible based recover 12 Step program) because I had so many issuesin my life that I didn't know how to deal with. Through this program God has been cleaning up my heart, healing my emotions and training me up for the work he has for me to do.

After several years of hard workI teamed up with my instructor (and friend) to help share this remarkable program with those who are really serious about changing their lifestyles and finding answers and healing.

I've now been drug and alcohol free for twenty-one years. I've seen God perform so many wonderful miracles, not only on my-self, but on others too and it still amazes me every time He does it!

He supernaturally opened a doorfor me to work at the Salvation Army Homeless Shelter for six years. A job that I was not qualified to be hired for, least wise not by man's standards, but

God wanted me there. I worked with all sorts of different people and was able to encourage and give hope to some of them that lived a life style much like my own.

Now, I have been working for The Champion's Centre for the last three years. The Champion Centre is a non-profit Christian organization that's set up for assisted living for men and I am their cook from Monday to Friday. We also have a program called the Hot Meal Program. We feed the homeless and the working poor on Saturday and Sunday, in which I also cook their meals. God has also opened the door for me to help minister the gospel through music and song in our local Remand Centre two times a month.

With that being said, when I look back over the years with the many trials and struggles I've faced, I shake my head in awe and thank Jesus for all He's brought me through. Truly He has taken me from the gutter to jail. I always felt like I came out of the gutter and now I'm going to jail two times a month to share the Gospel of Jesus Christ! There is no doubt about it, I am a walking miracle and to God be the Glory!

Barbra Valberg

October 8, 2009

Psalms 40:1, 2, 3a

I waited patiently for the Lord: He turned to me and heard my cry. He lifted me out of the slimy pit, out of the mud and mire: He set my feet on a rock and gave me a firm place to stand. He put a new song in my mouth, a hymn of praise to our God.

Miracle 54

God's Invisible Hands

My second son, Kevin, was born July 15, 1992. He was born with cancer but we didn't realize it until February but we didn't realize it until February 14, 1994 at 18 months old and passed away seven weeks later; to the day.

The doctors thought he had fluid on his brain. The hospital doctors called in a neurologist and found it to be tumors. By the time Kevin was 20 months old he had cancer all over in his tiny body.

The 9th of March he was coded; meaning he was put on a ventilator, respirator and the emergency equipment.

That is when I, Kevin's mother, was given the last time to hold my little boy, even though he was on a respirator. As I was rocking him, I told him, "Fight if you can, but if you have to go the Heaven to be with God, then it's OK.

You have fought so hard already". I then turned my heart and eyes up to Jesus and said, "If you need my baby more than me, please don't let my baby suffer any more".

Kevin had to have another Kemo treatment which meant that this Kemo treatment would possibly kill him but to not give him another treatment, meant he would surely die.

During Kevin's most serious time in the hospital, I recorded a tape with the song, "Stand by me", for little Kevin to listen to. I wanted so much to ease his pain and suffering and possibly make his journey easier.

The night before Kevin died, our cat, Sylvester, ran between the door and the bed in the bedroom. As she ran she howled intensively until I made like I was going out the door. But as soon as I went back to my bed and pulled up the covers, she would start screeching again!

Finally, I told Sylvester to lie down or I would put her in the kennel. Two hours later at 3:30 a.m. the next morning, I received a phone call from the hospital. Kevin was dying.

I went to the hospital and the doctor said I could talk to him. That is when I told my sweet baby, Kevin, that it was ok for him to go. Within a couple of minutes his little spirit was gone. Kevin had died.

I just sat, held his little hand, cried and sat.

Three hours later he was being readied for burial. I went to the gift shop and bought a pen and paper, sat down and wrote Kevin's eulogy and this is what I said;

A child is God's greatest gift. Their youth is not ours to have; but to borrow, so that we may re-experience the joys and sorrows of our own childhood.

Kevin was such a gift.

In the 20 months he was with us, he gave so much. He allowed us to see the wonderment of a world so pregnant with promise, hope and love.

Kevin taught us how to love one another, and how to show affection through the simplest gestures; be it a super juicy kiss, a warm, loving hug, an engaging, electrifying smile or a hearty robust laugh.

Through his illness, Kevin gave us perhaps the greatest gifts of all. He taught us how to embrace life, and how to savor the moments of joy and how to learn from our moments of sorrow. He also brought us all closer together, so that we would be able to cherish and remember what and how much we meant to each other.

Please, do not cry for Kevin, or be angry at the illness. God truly had a higher purpose for him; and now that Kevin has fulfilled his destiny, God has called him home; so that he may join the others who have gone before him in their peace and their work as very special Guardian Angels.

Lottie Gillmore

At the funeral I stood to give the eulogy while my Uncle stood behind me. He was a priest.

Within an instant prior to giving the eulogy, I lost all confidence to speak. Then all of sudden, I felt two adult size hands pushing me forward, holding me up on my back.

With that reassurance touch, I instantly knew I could do it.

When I finished, I stepped back and my Uncle gave me a loving hug. When I told my mom that I understand why my Uncle held me up, she said that no one touched me before or during the eulogy. That's when I new I had been strengthened supernaturally by the invisible hands of God. Yes, Jesus was present and He let me know it.

Life goes on

Life went back to somewhat normal. In 1996 Sue was stationed to Newbrunswick, Canada.

Before she had left to go there, she had found swollen, bumps on the back of her skull. The bumps grew as she was stationed in the army. An army official told her to go to the doctor. The base surgeon sent her to have a biopsy. The results came back as Non-Hodgkins Lymphoma-cancer of the Lymphodes.

She went to speak to the pastor of the army. She asked him to pray for her.

After six months of treatments, she lost all body hair, so she got a hat that said, "Bad hair day"!

She was off work for 1 ½ years. At 31 years old, in April, she finished treatments. On her 32 birthday Sue found out there was some cancer in her bone marrow. Both of her sisters had a dream that their bone marrow would match Sue's bone marrow. Both sisters' tests came back as complete matches.

Her younger sister, Jean, was chosen to donate the marrow. Twenty minutes after surgery, Sue went down to the 7-11 for a Coke-slush. Praise God!

Remember the story of David and Goliath? The pharmacist told while getting her prescription filled, told Sueit was almost impossible to receive good health again.

By the wonderful Grace of God, Sue has been cancer free for 12 years so far! She is another David and Praise Jesus, Cancer has been defeated! Thank you my precious Heavenly Father. Sue's bone marrow operation, for some unknown reason, had been scheduled for July 15, also the anniversary of her son Kevin's previous death years earlier.

Sue believes her sweet baby boy, somehow, was watching over her, her operation and her health outcome. Again, thank-you Father, God. Details fell beautifully into complete harmony.

Sue grew her hair out for 10 years. Her hair was down to her waist line. Then she cut it off and donated it to "Locks of Love", which is made into cancer patient's temporary hair. She makes knitted "Prayer Shawls, slippers, baby booties, hats and just about anything knitted asked for. They come in all colors, sizes, and shapes and she only takes donations for each item. The wool she buys with her own money and all the donations for her crafts go directlyto cancer research. She calls her handy-crafts, "Kevin's Comforts" in memory of Kevin, her baby son.

The Dream

A year after Kevin died I had a dream. In my dream, I was walking in a white hospital. People were walking in and out the door ways. I walked into one room and there was Kevin sitting on a bed.

That is when Kevin told me that he forgave me and that he loves me. He said that he is at peace and that he is fine.

By the Grace of God, my guilt has been forgiven and I am able to go forward in my life.

The Christmas Gift

The Christmas after Kevin died, Gerry was 5 years old. Gerry's preschool class wrote a letter to Santa Clause.

Previous to the letter, Gerry had told his mom that he wanted everything from the Sears Wish Book. Sue, his mother said that he should pick one gift for himself and one more gift for Kevin and give it to some sick boy or girl in the hospital.

He then sat down and asked his mom to help him write a letter to Santa. Gerry chose a small item for himself and a book for Kevin. He also asked Santa to ask God to give Kevin a hug and kiss from him.

Kevin's first words had been, Gee Gee, for Gerry, his big brother and now Gerry, even at 5 years old, felt the empty void of Kevin's absence.

The next morning, Gerry took the little letter to school with the intentions of sending it to Santa with the rest of his class-mates' letters. However, a few days later, Gerry came home in tears because when all the other children received letters back from the North Pole, there was none for him.

The next day, Sue received a phone call from the Deacon of the Catholic Church. The person on the other end of the phone stated that they had bought a gift as Gerry had requested but wanted Gerry's mother to know that no other child had asked Santa or God, to give a gift to another person besidesthemselves as Gerry had done.

The Church wrote a personal letter to Gerry and told him that Santa will be giving a sick child a gift and also that Santa asked God to give Kevin a hug and a kiss.

Gerry's Accident

We lived in Edmonton at the military base. It was 2007 and I, Susan, was at the time doing pre-deployment training for Afghanistan. I had been in the field training for two months when tragedy struck again!

I had come home from the field and decided to go to town for some chicken. Before I could leave to get the food, my phone rang and a lady said, "Do you have a son named Gerry"? "He's been hit by a car and it looks quite bad"!

Changed from my work clothes and went to the accident site.

There I found my son, Gerry, laying on the ground with blood all over his face. Gerry was very irritated! I tried to calm him. He said, "Mom, I lost my glasses, bank card and $5.45". Gerry was very distraught. And Gerry didn't have employment either.

It was Christmas time and a Christmas concert had just finished and was let out. Families were everywhere. They just stood there and stared as I watched the paramedics work on my son.

The woman that hit Gerry with her car was also watching him as he was slain on the road. While I was watching the paramedics work on Gerry, I kept clenching my hands, rubbing them firmly, over and over again. People offered me gloves but I could only say, "NO". I had to clench and wring my hands so I wouldn't interfere.

Finally the emergency paramedics were able to take Gerry to the hospital. A neighbor drove my car there and I road in the ambulance with my son. Gerry was strapped to a spine board. He had severe scrapes all over his head.

At the hospital the ex-rays came back and it indicated that the driver was going about 60 Km when she hit Gerry. She had been driving a Honda Civic.

As she floored the car, Gerry went into the windshield and left an indentation on the hood. She broke 5 vertebras in Gerry's back. Thank you Jesus, that Gerry had no spinal cord damage. His one knee was sprained but not broken. There were lacerations on his face and stitches on his forehead and back of his head.

At midnight, in the hospital, he got off of the spinal board. Nurses got me a reclining chair and I slept for then next2 hours.

Totally amazed and by a miracle of God, three days after the accident, Gerry walked out of the hospital, on his own.

Gerry needed a bed so we ordered a recliner chair for him.

Gerry's class room came to visit himin our home on one of their field trips. Gerry's Grandma and grandpa, Aunties and families and friends stopped everything to come and see Gerry while he was healing.

After the Christmas holidays, Gerry continued going to school like everyone else the beginning of January.

Mother, Sister, Daughter

Cancer Survivor

And Believer

In God we Trust

Thank you Jesus

Miracle 55

Angels at Work

---

86 year old man with a heart condition was having severe heart pains one night at home.

His wife asked, "Should I phone 911"!? He said, "No, not yet".

A few moments later their phone rang. It was 911 calling, asking it they needed an ambulance.

The elderly man said, "Yes, you better come".

After the ambulance got the man to the hospital, the man had a heart attack. Praise The Lord that man was at the hospital when the attack took place. He got through it and was eventually sent back home.

After the gentleman got home from the hospital stay, he checked to see if someone had called 911 the night beforethey had called him at his residence.

Quite amazingly, there was no recordof a phone call either way, from or to his house that evening. How was this possible? There seems to be no logical answer. This man is a born again believer in the Holy Trinity and truly believes in God's Angels. He believes that somehow, someway, his life was saved by God's Angels.

Anonymous,

Friend, in Christ

Miracle 56

Spiritual Warfare

I'm just a lonely soldier trying to hide

Looking for friends behind enemy lines

The world looks at me with
their superficial eyes

Judging and tormenting me
with their abusive lies

Everything revealed at Calvary

The most essential importantpoint
of victory

Trying to stand firm instead of to fall

Knowing defeat might be around
the corner we still crawl

Attacks coming at all sides

Like a beautiful vessel
fighting the tides

Always keeping your eyes on the prize

While the poor get stepped on

Inside my mind hearing
the children's cries

Which path to take the evil or good?

Righteous of course, it'sall
I ever could

The coward will always
play with your mind

Jesus rebukes you: that's howwe
deal with his kind

Lying spirits always making
a turmoil mess

Grab your Bible and read scripture
soldier, that's my guess

The Angel of Light trying to deceiveThe

Holy Ghost is all you
need to receive

God always gives glory to the Christ

Cost of getting to the Kingdom
of Heaven, just believe,

Is the price

So, let all my Christian brothers
and sisters cry out
All at once
DEATH TO THE FLESH
Shoot for home
With the Lord of the Heavens and
Complete the quest

This is for Long Sufferers
in Jesus Christ Name.
Spiritual Blessings for everyone!
Corey Douglas Myles
September, 2009

Miracle 57

By Prayer and the Grace of God

We have three children. Our youngest daughter, JoAnne, had chronic pneumonia as a young child.

When she was 5 years old, on a Sunday night, I, her mother, went to church and her dad, Charlie, stayed home with JoAnne.

When the time of prayer, at the Alter came, I went forward and a good friend of ours, named Louise, prayed an amazing prayer over me for our daughter, JoAnne.

Driving home, the thought kept coming to me to look at my scripture verse for the day. On arrival of getting home, I looked at my daily scripture verse and there I read: "Fear NOT: the child shall be made whole".

Now, by that powerful prayer at the Alter and the Grace of God Almighty, our 33 year old, baby daughter, since that night, has never had pneumonia again.

Priscilla

Mother, Wife and Daughter

And Believer in Power
of the Holy Trinity

In the Name of Jesus Christ

Miracle 58

Mystery Small Car

I was driving in winter, after dark to Claresholme, Alberta. I came to just past Lethbridge and had to chose firstor second side road to turn off on to Lethbridge. A few flakes of snow were coming down. Decided it was safe to keep going, so I took the side road that was shorter. Got part way down the back road and there was right around me a white out.

I was crying and scared. I sat there and cried out, "Jesus, Jesus, Jesus" as a call for help.

A truck came up behind me who was very impatient with me so I moved my car slightly over to the right and put on my 4 way flashers. The impatient truck roared very quickly past me.

When the truck had passed, I noticeda small car behind him. The small car stopped close behind me and just waited. While I examined the small car, a real sense of Peace seemed to come over me. I stopped crying, gathered myself emotionally, and felt safe in a very unsafe weather driving condition.

I slowly, with the small car behind me, drove until I could turn onto the #2 highway. The car followed me all the way to entrance to Claresholm. As I turned onto the road leading me into safety of a town, I turned to wave my thanks and where there, for miles, was a small car, was no one, no car, no sign of any one. There was no vehicle around. I had incredible Peace and I believe the phantom car was an Angel from God, to guide me to safety.

Sarah

Active Participant and
Believer in Jesus
Christ

Miracle 59

Carollyne and Brody May 8, 2009

May 7 "Our Daily Bread says,

"The difference Prayer makes"

Carollyne went into labor about 11:30 p.m. on May 7. Her water broke and she had some labor pains. Because her last delivery with Brooklyn was so fast we went to the hospital.

May 8 "Our Daily Bread says,

In every bad experience"

A young nurse examines her, puts her on the monitor and then tells her to walk around for a while since she was in very early labor. Nurse said she should send her home to come back later but wants her to stay because she says she just has a feeling. Another lady we met 2 days later was further in her labor and came in at the same time but was sent home and told to come back when her pains were 2-3 minutes apart. (God's first intervention)

All night Care's labor is progressing, but slowly. She is getting very tired and the nurse says she is not progressing like she should be. When it seems to have stopped she said it should hopefully start again later after she rests. Again she keeps her here instead of sending her home, because she just had a feeling. She had Care lie down in bed and just attempt to sleep to rest before it started up again. About 5 a.m. the nurse came in to check her again and Care said she had no labor pains but felt like her stomach was stretching so much it felt like it was ripping or tearing inside. The baby had moved and she was presenting very forward. As with all babies, so the nurse figured, was because Brody was moving down into position for birthing, therefore causing Care to have this tight stretching, tearing feeling. Other than that Care had no pain. The nurse tried to get a heartbeat on the monitor as Care was having a few contractions. The nurse told us that the babies heartbeat should be speeding up during a contraction but his wasn't. The nurse figured that Brody, the baby, must be sleeping – which most babies do before labor, to rest up. She got Care to change her position and then she had her get up and walk for a while to see if we could wake him and bring on more labor.

I was with Care while Jeff was sleeping in the chair in the corner. We let him sleep because he had a final exam for his second year of carpentry in the morning which he had to write. It's funny because in our minds we thought that Care would have Brody in a few hours from being admitted and Jeff could go write his exam. In a few hours he could come back and be with his now complete family. He had been studying most of the night since Cares labor had stopped and later fell asleep reading, so we just covered him up and left him to rest.

The nurse decided to call in the Doctor around 6 a.m. and she told him everything. He said he would shower and come in, in about 20 minutes, ashe wasn't too concerned.

The nurse came back and Sat with Care and I. I was watching the monitor for Brody's heart beat and Care's contractions. She left the room and then came right back – we didn't know till after that she had called the doctor and told him to come in ASAP.

He got there, it seemed like a few minutes later and he checked the monitor. The Doctor asked Care some questions and then did an internal. They decided to put a probe into Brody's headfor a more accurate reading as to whatwas going on with him. Then they told Care that they thought that it was bestif they did a C-section to help get babyout soon. I woke up Jeff at this time and told him they were taking her for a C-section and they were telling Care and Jeff about the options for him to be a part of the delivery and be by herside.

There did not seem to be a "real" urgency at this time. Then the Doctor left the room. The nurse was having Care sign consent papers and another nurse was taking her vitals. Meanwhile Care decided against the epidural. While Care was talking to Jeff I quickly called my husband at home and told him to come now. He came and brought Tanner, our youngest son, who was just leavingto go to work. I then hung up and calledLora our oldest daughter (who was at home with her three children and was expecting their fourth child within the month) what was going on. Her husband, Kris, dropped her off immediately at the hospital.

Meanwhile, Care was in bed waiting for the Doctor to come back, which he did. When he looked at the monitor he asked the nurse to confirm that the heart beat was not Care's on the monitor. I knew instantly by his voice and their conversation that there was definite urgency now. The nurse checked again and then said that it was Care's heart beat and it was weak, but where was Brody's then?

Then all of a sudden the Doctor yelled: "LET'S GO NOW!!!! WE DON'T HAVE TIME..." The doctor grabbed the head of her bed and the nurse grabbed the foot of her bed and some other people, I'm not sure if they were there before or not, grabbed the other areas of the bed. Everything happened so fast!I just had time to say "I love you". Her dad was just coming in the room with Tanner and he just had time to kiss herand say the same, as did Tanner. As I looked around at Jeff, my husband, Jim, Lora and Tanner, I knew we were all in shock and had no idea what was truly going on.

They ran down the hall to the operating room. I remember the Doctor yelling at a nurse at the nurse's desk to "GET THE PEDETRITION ON THE FLOOR NOW"!!! We stood there as if in slow motion listening and watching the staff as they quickly went about their tasksin a controlled panic.

We had no idea what was going on except that we were told by the Doctor, when he originally suggested the C-section that they thought Brody would do better if they got him out with help. He was getting stressed with the labor. We heard over the announcements, a code for something for NICU. There were people coming around the corner and going in thru the NICU and in thru the OR door. They told Jeff to just sit in the corner outside the OR door and they would update him. So there he sat with his yellow gown in the corner not knowing what was going on and separated from us as he was waiting just outside the OR doors. We were told to stay in the waiting room. A nurse told us that they would stop, so we could see Care, when they were taking her to recover. We all sat out in the hall, some pacing, some of us just sitting there. I went to hug and speak to Tanner, Lora and Jim and then I had to walk around. I was praying in the Spirit and I was praying for everything to be alright. I was numb and not even sure what to pray for.

Just then the Pediatrician came running down the hall towards the NICU. I called out and asked if she was going to see baby, just born? I said that's my grandson! She just squeezed my hand and said, "Ok". However, the look she had on her face was that of great concern.

Little did we know what was going on behind the walls literally, just feet from where we were all standing and sitting? I seemed like forever that we were waiting there. Then a social worker came up tous and introduced herself to us. She told us she would find out an up date for us. When she came back, she gathered us together and told us that there were some complications with Care and they are just taking a little longer with her. She said they would stop by the waiting room for us to see her, on their way to the recovery room. She told us she was just updating the happenings and checked on Jeff as well.

She said that Brody was born and that he was in the NICU being attended to. She said that Jeff was by his side. She said that as soon as she knew more she would come and tell us. She asked us if we needed anything and tried to make sure we were all looked after.

Meanwhile, Jeff was inside the Neo Natal Unit with Brody and they were working on him there. I felt so bad for Jeff dealing with all this by himself. At least we had each other. I needed to move around and pray and as I went around the corner I felt this strong need to call my church office. I just felt that Care and Brody needed more than our prayers. I just felt bigger than we could handle alone. I called the office and I told her only what I knew, which was not much. She said she would send out prayers on the prayer chain.

Now another Pediatrician was running towards the NICU. I did not know that our daughter, Lora, had called his office to tell him about Brody. He came right away to see Brody.

He hugged Lora, reassured her and told her he would check on everything and get back to her as quickly as possible. Time passed slowly. The Social Worker comes back and tells us that the Doctor is still with Care and that Brody is still being attended to. The Pediatrician is on the phone with Calgary, NICU, conferring with them.

Somewhere in there, I phoned our oldest son, Karl, in Calgary and told him what was going on and to pray for both, Care and Brody. Without telling us, he was now leaving work and going to drive here to be with his sister and us. I also had phoned my mom, my brother and my sister to tell them all what was happening and to pray. I was concerned that my mom would have too much stress, so I did not tell her everything. Kris, Lora's husband went over to pick up my mom who had been at Care's house since 11:00 p.m., watching Brooklyn since we had gone into the hospital the night before. He was to bring her to her own home and make sure she was ok.

I phoned Kelly at work to tell her to pray. She told the staff on the first floor at City Hall and many of them begun to pray as well. This all seemed to happen over a few minutes.

Jeff had come in and out of the room with bits of information but he wasn't making a lot of sense to us because he was so upset. He would not finish his sentences, saying just bits and pieces of information. I think they had told him so much he was trying to absorb it all and his brain was racing. He was saying something about his Brody's lungs and brain and being air lifted to Calgary...He needed to keep some air and to think and he needed to call his mom. That's when Tanner went with him for a walk in the halls to make sure he was alright, talking to him and trying to calm him down. Then Jeff would go back in the NICU again. Tanner was watching for him each time he came out of the NICU and went to be with him. We still did not know about Care yet.

Then the doors opened and they were quickly wheeling Care out of the OR and into the recovery room. We knew immediately that something was wrong because they blew right past us and never even acknowledged us standing there. She looked like she was dead, as cold as that sounds. That was my first thought! She was so grey and cold looking and so lifeless. Lora grabbed one of the nurses following behind Care that she recognized and told the nurse that that was Carollyne that they were working on. She asked how Care was. The reply was something like, "We had to close her up so quickly. We have to take a special X-Ray, just to make sure we didn't leave any instruments inside her. She has lost a lot of blood. And as soon as she is stable we'll let you know"! We just stood there in silence, not believing what we had just heard. As soon as she is stable?! Closed her up so quickly?! What was going on?!!

Lora stood outside that door with her nose press against the glass window just watching as they worked on Care in the recovery room. She was updating Tanner and me. She said that when the nurse looked at her, she then closed the curtain so she could not see them working on Care. Lora was pregnant as well, just about 3-4 weeks behind Care and was starting to have labor pains from the stress. When the Social Worker just happened to be looking for us, tosee how we were doing, she noticed Lora and she got a chair for her to sit in. She was trying to reassure Lora and she wanted her to go for a stress test but Lora said she was not leaving the door until she knew Carollyne was ok. She sat at that door and just stared at it with Tanner by her side. It still breaks my heart when I think back to seeing the two of them standing there just waiting for any bit of information on their sister. Jeff would come out from seeing Brody and also was waiting for word on his wife. My husband sat around the corner in the waiting room, looking lost and empty with his head in his hands.

I wondered quickly how Karl was handlingit in Calgary by himself and my mom ather apartment. But there was no time to think much more than that, as our concern at the hospital was Carollyne,Brody and Jeff.

We saw another Pediatrician come out of the NICU and I approached him in the hall. I asked him about Brody and he told me that he was a very sick little boy. He said that his Pediatrician was still on the phone with Calgary and she would talk to the family soon. That was the most information we had had so faron Brody. I could not even think aboutwhat our little grandson was going thru in there!

The Social Worker came back and told us that Care had lost lots of blood, almost 6 units, which apparently ishalf of your blood supply. She would either be going to a room on maternity or to ICU? She said if Cara went to the maternity ward she would still not be out of the woods but it would be much better than ICU.

She told us that Brody might have to be airlifted to Calgary. The Doctor wasn't sure yet. They would update us on his status real soon. What was going on? Lord, give us the strength to deal with this. Lord, Jesus, give us your peace that surpasses all understanding and loose the power of your HOLY SPIRIT into this whole situation!

Some time much later, someone came out and told us that Care would be taken down to a room on the maternity floor. Thank GOD!! Tanner took all the bags from her labor room down to the maternity room. When Care came out of the recovery room she looked like she was definitely on deaths door. She actually looked worse then when they flew by us from the operating room as they took her to her room. She was heavily sedated and did not even know we were there. Jeff was with her when they brought her down to her room and once they had her settled in her room, while she was in and out of her sedation, he told her about Brody, that he was going to be airlifted to Calgary.

In a, groggy, response she told Jeff, that he needed to be with Brody so that he wasn't alone up there.

Carollyne was not out of the woods yet, as they were worried that she would go into shock from the large loss of blood.

While Jeff was with Care, Jim, Lora, Tanner and I got to go in and see Brody briefly. He was so beautiful. It must have been the look in our eyes that his nurse saw that se began to explain to us what all the wires and tubes were that were sticking out of him. Even writing this now, it is so over whelming. To walk in and see what we saw. He was so little. He looked so perfect and yet he was inso much distress.

We saw the Pediatrician on the phone just feet from his wee bed and she was still in conversation with a Doctor in Calgary about Brody. We watched his nurse tenderly speak and work on him. They were constantly monitoring his vitals while it seems that he was hooked up to so many machines.

We were asked to not even touch him as it would stimulate his little body too much. They were trying to lower his body temperature. I can't remember how low they needed it to go, but it was to slow down any further damage to his vital organs.

Newborn baby's should be swathed tightly and held in your arms so that they can feel your warmth and love.

Here Brody lay on his wee bed with only a diaper on, with no blankets, with no swaddling, with no loving arms able to hold him to reassure him, to comfort him, to kiss his little hands and head, to tell him it will all be ok. Jeff watched them hook him up to the machines. He listened to them talking, while they carried out their life saving tasks on him, all the while unable to do anything at all for Brody, but watch. The whole time he was wondering, not knowing what was going on with his wife in the next room. WOW.

I was and still am so proud of him for his strength and his courage.

Then, Brody's Pediatrician and Calgary NICU decided that in order to prevent any more damage to Brody's organs, he needed to be kept on a cooling pad for up to 72 hours, to lower his body temperature and to slow down any damage.

They could not do it here in Medicine Hat Hospital and that was the reason they were air lifting Brody to Calgary.

Because they did not have the equipment to stop any further damage from happening in his little body, he was flown out. Apparently, when you have no oxygen circulating in your body, your extremities loose it first, then all your organs, with I think the brain and the heart being the last and then it's death to the body.

Brody, we were told was born with out breathing or a heartbeat and they had no idea for how long he went without. The test they performed and the levels that came back from his test showed that it was for quite a while for not breathingor heartbeat. He was in bad shape. They were concerned about his kidneys andat the time while we were there, also his brain and how much damage he had sustained.

Care was insistent when she was alert for a few minutes, that Jeff leave her to be there when Brody arrived in Calgary. She needed to know that their son was not alone up there in Calgary. She at this point had no idea of what she had gone through herself and the danger that she was still in. She just assumed it wasa routine C-Section that she had had. Jeff was torn between Care and Brody, but we reassured him that we would not leave Carollyne's side. We said that he should go to be there when Brody arrived at the Calgary hospital.

This way he could up date Care through out the day and night on Brody's progress and as soon as she was able, she would beright up there by both their sides, withBrooklyn.

I phoned my son, Karl, who wasjust getting ready to leave Calgary to come to the Hat and asked him to stay there and be there for Jeff and Brody. He went to the hospital and waited forboth to arrive. Jeff had to drive up whileBrody was airlifted. The Social Worker arranged for his parking and for some meal tickets to help him out at the hospital. I then phoned Kris (Russell), he is like a third brother to my children and told him what was going on with Care and Brody. He was in Red Deer training when I called and before 5 o'clock that day, he was at the hospital with Karl waiting for Jeff and Brody to arrive. I knew he'd look out for both Jeff and Karl. The boys, Karl and Kris, stayed by Jeff's side and stayed for each day till we got up there the next Tuesday.

Before Jeff left for Calgary, the nurses decided to wheel Carollyne's bed from the maternity ward in the NICU to see Brody for the first time, before he was airlifted. She was still so heavily sedated that she was unable to sit up, because of being heavily sedated and her incision. She really had no idea what was going on-even though Jeff had tried to tell her in her room earlier. She only could see his little foot as she looked up from her bed to his wee bed. She reached up and touched his little foot. She had not seen her baby yet and they were going to take him away. It was heart breaking when she asked in a real groggy voice, to the nurse, "Could you tell me why is he here? What's wrong with him"? The whole room had tears. So Brody's NICU nurse started to explain it to Care. There in the NICU room, besides Care, Jeff and Brody, was Lora, her husband

Kris, Tanner, Jim, two Pediatricians, Care's Doctor and the Airlift crew from the Calgary NICU, as well as me. After this touching moment and first visit of mom and son, they wheeled Care backto her room to rest, so they could finish getting Brody ready to be airlifted out. Jeff spent more time with Care and then went home to pack and then was on his way also.

Because Care was so sedated when they wheeled her down to the NICU, just before they airlifted Brody out, it was so compassionate of the NICU nurses and NICU-Calgary nurses who would be flying back with Brody, to stop into Carollyne's room this time, so mom could see baby, one more time. Again her grey hand touched his little tummy but she did not get to see him. His high incubator and her inability to sit up with her medical state, did not allow her to see him, but only to just reach up and touch him. Lora and Kris, Tanner and Jenna, Jim and I were all present and again, so impacted by this very special moment once again.

Before Jeff left to go to Calgary he stopped in to talk to his teacher at the college and tell him what was going on. He was so understanding and supportive. Jeff would be given a re-write and would not be penalized. He did write his exam at a later date and passed.

Brody was then airlifted. Jeff was close to Calgary and Karl and Kris were waiting for the two to arrive. I stayed at the hospital with Care until she was discharged.

May 10, Daily Bread says
Childlike Faith

The Doctor on call on the second day, told us she was not out of the woods yet. They were worried that her body would go into shock from so much blood loss or that she would start to bleed again. On the second day she received 3 units of blood to help her get up and out of the hospital sooner so that she could be with Brody, Jeff and Brooklyn.

Carollyne needed 6 units of blood, she received 3. We are scared to death of blood transfusions and all the risks and fears that goes with it. We prayed that the blood she is about to receive wouldbe free from any form of reactions or from any form of disease present in itnow or in the future. We prayed for a Peace to be upon us with our decisionand there it was, God's Peace.

On Friday afternoon, Carollynes best friend, Jen was on her way down fora visit from Calgary. Once she heard about Carollyne, she stopped in to see Care right away, in the late afternoon. Although I don't think Care even knew Jen was there, Jen just sat by her side watching her sleep. Jen came back again on Saturday and Sunday to sit with Care for a few hours. When she went back to Calgary she visited Jeff and Brody and did what she could for Jeff.

I called my friend Janet that morning of the 8th and she called me later that day to see how things were going. We prayed on the phone. She called me back about half and hour later and said she was praying when GOD told her to come to the hospital, so we could pray together. We went to the hospital Chapel. We got on the floor there and just went into prayer for both Care and Brody. GOD gave us scripture after Scripture and we prayed more. Then we started laughing and I knew it was my confirmation of what I already knew... "It is Done". Thank you LORD!!!

I told Care when I got back to the room and she was very quiet but said she felt the same thing. She just knew everything was going to be ok.

The next day Carol, Pastor Ken's wife, came up to see Care. She stayed for a while, just listening. She was there when the Doctor came in and talked to Care, confirming all that had happened. When she prayed with us before she left it was the first time Care had cried.

My mom came by and just sat with Care, got her a warm blanket and just watched her sleep, as I caught up on my sleep beside her, on the cot. Bob, Nic, Joshua and Frannie, my brother, sister-in-law, nephew and sister, all came to check on Care. Sometimes a phone call is just not enough. Loved ones have to see you. It's just such a helpless feeling.

Care's Doctor came in to see her and he asked her if she understood what really had happened to her and to Brody. He told her she was seconds from death and said that when the Doctor opened her up to do the C-Section, he had no idea that there was that much blood that had leaked into behind the placenta area. There was only a little bit of placenta attached to the wall and in this situation most women would have bled out but she bled in. Therefore nobody had any idea what was going on with her. When the Doctor cut her open he had a major life threatening situation that he had to deal with. If he had waited even another few seconds, he would have lost them both.

They had no idea how long Brody had no oxygen because of the pulled away placenta, but they knew that it was for a while. While the Doctor was trying to stop Care from hemorrhaging and dying in front of him, a nurse from NICU was doing 3 minutes of chest compression trying to revive Brody. This had all happened so quickly that the Pediatrician had not even made it there yet. We were told afterwards that in charge did everything right!! GOD is in the house and was working on both Brody and Carollyne.

Sunday, May 10 Our Daily Bread saysMothers and Magnets Mother's Day

Jeff is still in Calgary with Brody. He checks with Brody's nurse and his tests for later that day has been cancelled till the next day. He decides to surprise Carollyne so he drives down from Calgary to the Medicine Hat to spend Mother's Day with her and his daughter, Brooklyn.

They spent half the time together and then Jeff went and picked up Brooklyn to bring her to the Hospital to see her mommy for the first time since Brody's birth. This was the best present Carollyne could ever get on Mother's Day. Jeff looked exhausted. He needed to leave at 4:00 a.m. to get back to the Calgary Hospital to be there for Brody's next test the next day. So as short of a visit it was, it was badly needed for them all. What an awesome surprise it was!

Monday, May 11 Our Daily Bread Says

The World is Watching

Meanwhile, Lora has been dealing with a deluge of calls from family and friends, asking about Carollyne and Brody. Her house phone and cell phone mailboxes had been filled up, as was our house phone. Lora decided to make up a Facebook page on Care and Brody's Story and before long it had a few hundred entries with prayer's and word's of encouragement.

Lora updates the site every day, sometimes twice a day, on both Brody and Carollyne. It keeps her busy and it reassures our family and friend's while it gives us the privacy that we need. Care and I both knew that Lora wanted to be by her side the whole time but with three small children of her own at home, expecting another baby in three to four weeks and watching, Care and Jeff's daughter, Brooklyn, she had her hands full. Through the whole time though, her heart was in the hospital. She called and visited her sister as much as she was able. I thought of her often, wondering how she was dealing with all of it.

Jeff works for Advance Design and Construction in Medicine Hat. And Carollyne works for the Royal Bank down town and for the City during Tiger Games and other Arena functions. These companies, co-workers and friends were so concerned and supportive.

They all showed them so much love and concern and blessed them over the top. Care and Jeff were over whelmed after the fact of how much they are truly blessed, loved and cared for by their co-workers, friends and the companies they work for. On their behalf, I thank you all so much from the bottom of our hearts.

Tuesday, May 12 Our Daily Bread Says

Getting Better

On the Fifth day, a Tuesday, Care's Doctor released her from Medicine Hat Hospital against his better judgment but knew she needed to be with her baby, Brody, in Calgary. She promised to go straight home to pack and then to Calgary and that she would rest. I told him I was going to look after Care and Brooklyn and I would make sure that Care rested. Within two hours of being released, Brooklyn, Care and I were on our way to Calgary Hospital. On our way out of the hospital, the day could not have been more beautiful, sunny, slight breeze, and birds singing. It was amazing! I said to Care that if GOD hadn't intervened into her situation and Brody's situation that today would have been her funeral and his funeral. We were silent for a moment. I apologized for what I had said and how it sounded, but everything had just come into perspective and it was so evident to the both of us. A definite, a-hah, moment, for me! GOD is so GOOD!! And we were so blessed!

Before we left for Calgary, while Care was packing her clothes, her cell phone rang and it was the NICU nurse that was watching over Brody. Her reason for calling Care was to tell Care that, "If you don't believe in GOD or Miracles, you had better start because in front of her was nothing short of a Miracle"! "Brody was not the same baby that came in a few days ago and they could not explain it, other than a Miracle"!! WOW!!

As we left Medicine Hat, I found it hard to leave Lora and Tanner behind. Jim was already on the road once he knew Carollyne was going to be ok and was released. He knew he couldn't just hang around the hospital. He had to keep busy. If needed, he could be in Calgary in a few hours.

On our way up to Calgary, Care, Brooklyn and I were going to be put up in a hotel, single room, because Ronald McDonald house was full. Around Gleitan, a Social Worker called on

Care's cell phone to tell us that Ronald McDonald house had an opening for us after all. I was thinking to myself on the way up, of ways on how would I amuse Brooklyn, a three year old, in a hotel and pay for all the meals and a hotel room. They had offered us a special rate at the hotel, but now we would be staying at Ronald McDonald house with a full kitchen and play area plus centers for Brooklyn. If you ever wanted to give to a worthy cause, Ronald McDonald house would be an excellent choice and blessing to all those who ever have to stay there.

Care got to see and finally hold her baby once we got there. Care, Jeff, Brooklyn and Brody spent some alone time that, was a start of the healing process for all of them. Care spent many hours each day by his incubator with Jeff by her side. We were worried she wasn't getting the rest that she needed. Physically tired and emotionally drained, she spent as much time as possible by Brody's side. It was by his side that she realized that Jeff was sitting on a wooden stool each day, hour after hour, leaning on Brody's incubator, holding his little hand and talking to him. It was so evident that when Jeff spoke, little Brody's head would turn towards his Daddy's reassuring voice.

Care realized that she had so much support with her in Medicine Hat, and yet day after day Jeff sat by Brody on that stool watching and listening to every beep on the monitor as his son lay on a cooling (cold) mat unable to hold him or comfort him. Every time at shift change, he would phone Care and update her with Brody's progress and after each test and report he would call her as well. He took pictures on his cell phone and sent them to Care so she could actually see what Brody looked like. Kris and Karl sat in the waiting room waiting patiently for Jeff to come out of the NICU each day, so that whenever he left Brody, they were there for him. At the end of the day they would go home to Karl's place, to eat, sleep and do it all over again the next day. We were all thankful that Karl and Kris were there for Jeff, while Jeff was there for Brody.

Thursday, May 14 Daily Bread says "Making the Cut"

On Thursday, May 14, the day before his release, we were told Brody could possibly go home Friday after the Doctor/Specialist saw his test results of Brody's brain wave test? To discover if there was any permanent brain damage that was sustained during his traumatic birth. These were the last results we were waiting for. Every other test came back normal. His liver, kidney, heart, were all good and he had no seizures, was a surprise as they thought he would have many of them. The Doctor said he was a real fighter and that he was surprised at all the test results so far but that this test would tell us if he was going to have any brain damage.

Friday, May 15 Daily Bread

saysThe Secret is...

Care, Jeff and Brooklyn and me, were there when the Specialist came in the morning and he proceeded to tell us that he was a perfectly healthy baby boy. He said that every test they did on him was conclusive and that he suffered no injuries or permanent damage, not in his brain or in any of his organs. He said he had to check the results twice and can only say that it was nothing short of a miracle. I asked about Brody's future and he reassured us that "if" anything, he may have just the slightest learning disability "if" anything!! Praise GOD!!

Brody went up to Calgary on May 8th and he was released from Calgary NICU on May 15th, exactly 7 days later, well and healthy.

At the end of his stay in Calgary Hospital, he was ambulanced back to the Hat and we left soon to be there when he arrived.

It was a long ride home, a long time to think and absorb all that had happened over the past week. It gave us much time of reflection. Care rode with Jeff and I had Brooklyn with me.

The experiences we each had everyday showed us that GOD is and was in control every second of our journey. The day we were to leave I walked around Ronald McDonald house very early that morning and cried. Why were we so blessed and so many other children and parents had to still walk through their fire? You feel so blessed and at the same time, I felt so guilty for our blessings. GOD's ways are not our ways nor are his thoughts our thoughts. I can only receive what God has chosen to do for my family and thank him from the bottom of my heart – which is still not enough. I can only hope and pray that this whole situation has impacted, moved, changed and transformed each one of us into the people HE has created us to be. I pray that each one of us, through this ordeal, will begin to seek

HIM out to find our true GOD given destiny in HIM.

I wait in anticipation to see what GOD has in store for Carollyne and Brody, as you will read on for Dylan as well. If He has done this for them now, what does HE have in store for their futures?! It's so exciting to think about that prospect!

Back in the Hat

The nurses in the NICU and on the maternity floor in the Hat could not believe that Brody was coming back already and with a clean bill of health. He would just have to stay in the hospital till his birth weight was back to where it should be and Care was able to get him into a nursing (feeding) schedule.

Carollyne's nurses did not recognize her when she returned to floor (they gave her a rooming in room) to be close to Brody, who would be staying in the NICU. They were so surprised that she looked so good, all her color was back. She seemed to have lots of energy and it seemed as if nothing, "life- altering," had happened to her at all.

Brody's nurse was amazed at Brody's complete turn around and at Care's health turn around. She was the nurse who preformed the chest compressionfor three minutes to bring him back to life. To you, we are forever grateful!

To the Doctor who performed Carollyne's C-Section we also are forever grateful to you!

To the labor and delivery nurse who followed her "feeling", we are also eternally grateful to you!

To Brody's Pediatrician...Thank you for your wisdom in his treatment and for you, we are also forever grateful!

To Carollyne's Doctor, who was 20 minutes from coming off shift and it would have been too late to help either one...for your tears, for your compassion, for not leaving the NICU till Brody was on his way to Calgary. For your honesty, for being so real, (to bothmy girls), I thank you from the bottom of my heart! You made the difference in the two of my girls pregnancy's (all 6 of our grand children).

Brody's birth weight rose steadily and he was soon ready to go home. Together this family would need time to heal, time to reflect and time to connect again after being apart and going through so much. Care and Brody were both given a new lease on life. Thank you, GOD, again!!!

Another Miracle during this Situation

Care's Dad, Jim, while driving on his way to the Edmonton area on Monday morning was praying and lost in his thoughts. Suddenly a bird hit the grill of his car. He said that all of a sudden he heard GOD saying, "That bird just gave his life for Carollyne". Surprised at this statement, Jim said back to GOD in prayer, "If that bird gave his life for Care than why can't another bird give his life for Brody"? Within about ½ hour to 45 minutes later, another bird, smaller than the first, hit the side of his car.

This was such a spiritual moment for him, thinking that GOD cared enough to show up and be with him to reassure him that his daughter and grandson would be ok. He just knew because he knew! He travels all the time as part of his work, for many years and he figured what are the odds that two birds would hit his car in one day. Especially when he had just asked GOD for another bird to be sacrificed for Brody, after he heard GOD say that the first one was for Carollyne. He was blown away and had to pull over. He decided to call me and told me that something really spiritual had just happened to him and then he told me what it was. He knew it was all GOD telling him that both would be ok! He was at total peace after that.

GOD is always with us but it was so evident of that, from the second Care's water broke that HE was by Brody's and her side. HE had the whole situation in HIS control. HIS fingerprints are all over every minute of this situation.

I have tried to recall as much as I could to the best of my ability. This recap was written as I experienced it through my eyes and ears and from my heart. When I look back now and try to digest what we all went thru, I know that God's peace was upon us all. It seemed so surreal, as HE carried us through it all. This was so much like the "Footprints" poem.

We all had different angles as we were watching this whole situation unfold, from different feelings, different ways of dealing with it to different waysof expressing it. But one thing is for sure, it was all GOD!!! He used Amazingpeople with amazing gifts. HE, in His perfect timing used all of it, all together!HE was there for every Nurse, every Doctor, Social Worker, family member and all friends, in Medicine Hat, Calgary, Edmonton and Ottawa.

For ever prayer that was released, through tears, through whispers to unspoken hearts, GOD has used each and every one of you and we are forever and eternally grateful to you all. Like the nurse said to Carollyne on the phone from Calgary,

"If you don't believe in GOD or miracles, then you had better start"!

The Three-Month Devotional for March, April and May 2009

A few weeks after this whole ordeal, I picked up my copy of "Our Daily Bread". I decided to read the days of Brody's birth and the following days. It seemed that each day had a message for us and the titles of those pages are as follows.

Our Daily Bread

Seemed to follow us each day...

Wednesday, May 6 At Just the Right Time

Thursday, May 7   The Difference Prayer Makes

Friday, May 8   In every Bad Experience

(Brody born and air lifted to Calgary)

Saturday, May 9   Child like Faith

Sunday, May 10   Magnets and Mothers

Monday, May 11   The World is Watching

(Started for updates and prayers by

Lora) Face book page

Tuesday, May 12   Getting Better (Care Leaves Hospital)

Wednesday, May 13 Godly Sorrow

Thursday, May 14   Making the Cut

All Brody's Tests are so far "Normal"

Friday, May 15   The Secret is---

The day Brody came back to the Hat.

Notes

Every time the nurses or Doctors came in to tell us some "bad" news, we refused to accept it in our hearts and believe it. We just knew beyond the shadow of a doubt that Brody was going to be just fine in every way. They told us that he would have 2nd degree or second level brain damage. Because of his birth, they said he would have kidney, heart and brain damage and that he would have some form of Cerebral Palsy. We were told he would be up in Calgary for a few weeks and then be back in the Hat.

In Calgary at shift change, Care over heard the one nurse talking to the new shift nurse talking about his birth. She said that it took 3 minutes of chest compressions to bring him back. That was when we first found out how traumatic his birth really was. We remembered that, after the fact, they had told us in the Medicine Hat Hospital that he was born not breathing and had no heart beat hence all the problems with his organs and lungs. I think that we had information over load and when Care heard it again it really sunk in then.

1st Miracle	Carollynes life saved within second hemorrhaging to death
2nd Miracle	Brody brought back to life after three (GOD's perfect number) minutes of chest compressions
3rd Miracle	Brody is perfect. No damage, no long or short term effects. Doctors in Calgary can't explain his amazing recovery.
4th Miracle	GOD using two birds to speak to my husband.
5th Miracle	Ronald McDonald house calling us with opening.

Our Thoughts

Why didn't the nurse send Care home that night when she wasn't really in labor? She said she had a feeling… If this had happened at home at 6 a.m., in the morning she and Brody would have died for sure, as there would not have been any time to act and save them.

When Care's nurse made a 2nd phone call to the Doctor and told him to come, ASA P?

Nurse calls us from Calgary NICU to ask if we believe in miracles?

Doctor in Calgary NICU on Friday says he can't explain all the perfect test results, except for a miracle.

Birds, Jim's car and Jim talking with GOD.

The full witness of God's Miracle Power, on face book, to all or our family, friends and strangers. People all over Medicine Hat and areas were talking about Care and Brody and the Miracle.

Read On....

Three Weeks Later.........

Lora and Dylan Ruth

On June 16, 2009, a few weeks after Brody was home from the Medicine Hat Hospital, Lora was celebrating her own birthday, with a special surprise entrance from Dylan Ruth. Once again in the delivery room when things should be going smoothly with a normal delivery, we found ourselves once again, praying for God's intervention.

With so much stress from the ordeal of seeing what her sister, Care and nephew, Brody, went through, Lora just wanted to get through the rest of her pregnancy and delivery with no problems or issues.

In the hospital, she was focusing during her contractions on Dylan's heartbeat on the monitor, while her husband, Kris and I stood by for support. During her labor, things slowed down, so they started to induce her to help things along. It wasn't far into her labor after this that while in a strong contraction she sensed something was wrong. Within seconds, she decided that it was best for her to push Dylan out right away. As the nurse tried to tell her to stop pushing, that she wasn't yet fully dilated, Lora continued to push with all her might. Kris and I just stood by wondering what the heck was going on!

While Dylan was forcibly entering the world, the nurse was preparing for her to arrive. As soon as she was born, we were all standing around admiring her but also waiting for those first cries that always sound so sweet to any ears.

The nurse tried frantically to get her to breath but to no avail. It seemed to take forever but I'm sure it was within minutes, the room was filled with other nurses and doctors. They moved Dylanto her wee bed that they had set up andthey went frantically to work on her, getting her to breath her first breath.

I thought to myself, "Oh NO LORD, NOT AGAIN"!! With Brody we were separated by walls and knew nothing that was going on. This time I was inches from my daughter's side, feet from her husband, Kris and we were in the middle of it all.

I was so grateful for everyone in the room. And again it was a controlled panic going on. Once again we all felt so helpless as we just stood motionless and watched and waited for her tiny body to take her first breath. I was tryingto focus on my daughter, who looked like she was going into shock as she tried to see her daughter through all the nurse's and doctor's working on her. We could just hear them talking back and forth, shouting out instructions andcommands.

From the first second I realized there was a problem, I found my self praying for GOD to once again intervene into our situation. I don't remember my words but my heart was praying volumes. I quickly went to the hall to tell Jim that Dylan was born but to pray, as she was not breathing. He had been in the waiting room awaiting the birth of another grandchild, number 6 for us. When he heard Lora's screams and saw the rush of medical staff to her room, he stood outside just waiting for news on what was happening.

When they starting bagging Dylan with air or oxygen, I'm not sure and breathing for her, I was relieved just knowing that some oxygen was getting into her brain and her little purple body. I looked over and at one time, Kris was filming the birth and not knowing what was going on he continued to film them trying to resuscitate his little girl. He followed them over to her little bed. I'm not sure when it hit him but, all of a sudden, he threw the camera onto the chair and looked over at Lora. He now looked like he was in shock. This had all happened so quickly, really none of us knew until they moved her to the little bed that this was very serious. As they bagged her, I believe it was about 15 minutes after her birth that she began to breath, on her own. THANK GOD!!!

As they cleaned her up and checked her over from head to toe, before they took her to NICU for observation and to be checked, they let Lora and Kris hold their precious little miracle bundle. Jim was out in the hall listening to the whole ordeal. I was trapped in the corner trying to stay out of the way so I could not make it to tell Jim that she was finally ok. As I finally went out in the hall to inform him of what had just happened and that she was finally breathing, we just kind of melted into each other arms and started to cry. Then Jim came in and held onto little Dylan and gave Loraa big hug.

She is fine today with no problems at all. She is a beautiful, healthy, little girl.

Once again, we're not sure what happened or why it happened but we all believe that GOD's intervention saved our little Dylan. She spent a week in the NICU for observation while Lora roomed in which, was the same room that Care roomed in, while Brody was in NICU.

Later, when I asked why she (Lora) had decided to push Dylan out early, before she was fully dilated, Lora told them what had happened.

She spoke of concentrating on the fetal heartbeat on the monitor during her contractions to help her deal with the pain. When she had had a very strong and strange contraction, she noticed that the heartbeat had disappeared and could not be heard. No one else in the room noticed that, that, at all. Her next contraction was almost immediate and Lora could not hear the heart beat again. She said that after everything that Care had gone through with Brody, all she could think of was getting Dylan out, that she was in trouble! The Doctor checked the print out after, on the fetal heart machine, and he confirmed Lora's assumption...the heartbeat had stopped. He told her that it might have been a different ending for Dylan if she had not been born when she was. Lora said she just had a strong feeling that something was wrong and she said she knew that if she had to explain what she felt and what she sensed, to the nurse, it would be valuable time that Dylan did not have. So she said she just knew she had to get her baby born. This she did even though it could have caused her serious problems delivering before she was fully dilated. Lora already has three children and has issues with hemorrhaging after her births. She classed as a high-risk pregnancy. By doing what she did, she really risked her own life by pushing Dylan out before she was fully dilated.

Dylan was kept in the NICU unit for seven days before Lora was released from the hospital, same number of days as Brody in Calgary.

This family has experienced so many touches from GOD in so many areas of our lives. Once again, no actually twice again, now he has shown HIS Love, HIS

Mercy and HIS Grace to each one of us, especially to Carollyne, Brody, Dylan and Lora.

Again, this is all to my recollection and to the best of my ability, from my memory.

Once again, we all had different angles that we were watching both of these situations unfold from, different feelings, different ways of dealing with it and different ways of expressing it.

But one thing is for sure. It was all GOD!!! He used Amazing people with Amazing gifts and talents. HE, in his Perfect timing used ALL of it, all together, to work for HIS glory with every Nurse, every Doctor, every Social Worker, All of our Family, Friends, Co-Worker's and Strangers in Medicine Hat and distant family in Calgary, Edmonton and in Ottawa, Thunder Bay and New Orleans. For every prayer that was released, through tears, through whispers, through unspoken hearts, through Praise and through Worship, GOD has used each and every one of you!!!

May GOD FOREVER BLESS You
and
Keep You under HIS Wings!!!

Danielle Williams

Miracle Making Invitation

Now that GOD has touched your life with many miracles of other's around you, He wants you to know that more miracles are on the way, daily, possibly for you and your loved one's.

If you want to know Jesus Christ, our Living God, as your Personal Savior and have your name written in the Book of Lambs, as GOD's chosen Saints, up in Heaven, then now is the time to sincerely ask GOD to forgive you, of all your sins. Sincerely ask Jesus Christ into your heart and ask Him to wash your heart as white as snow, with the bloodof Jesus, the Lamb.

GOD cannot lie! His Holy Word say's that He is Faithful to cleanse us of our sins when we sincerely ask Himfor forgiveness and ask Jesus into our hearts. GOD loves each person! That means YOU, with all HIS heart! His word say's that He will never leave us nor forsake us!

If you need a miracle in your life, whether mental, physical, family-wise, relationship-wise, addiction-wise, money-wise, spiritual-wise or anything else-wise, know GOD is in the MIRACLE business and know also that He wants to show YOU what HE does best!!

Trust Him. Ask Jesus into your heart. Then run, DON'T walk, and share what you just did with someone, of the Greatest Decision that you have EVER made, in your life!! That being to follow, Jesus, as your Personal Lord and Savior.

Read His Holy Word. Read for your selves, all the wonderful promises that GOD has, waiting, for you and me, in our Christian, daily walk. Join a Holy Trinity Believing, Spirit fed and Alive Church and as you walk with Jesus, Father GOD, and His Holy Spirit; you will reap the rewards of abundant adventure and fulfillment, like never before in your life experiences!

Conclusion

Thank you for walking with me through this amazing book of, "People's Personal Miracles in Medicine Hat". I hope and pray that your lives were touched, blessed and possibly changed by GOD's Glory as He was revealed to us through personal, story after story.

And to all of you, very special Children of GOD, that were led by GOD's HOLY SPIRIT to share your true Miracle encounters: THANK YOU, from the bottom of my heart. My sincere prayer for each one of you is this, "May Jesus, GOD the Father and His Holy Spirit, continue to lead you, guide you, bless you, reward you and make your paths straight and smooth while covering you with HIS Presence. May you always be well and healthy, in your Mind, Body, Soul and Spirit. And may our Heavenly Father continue to use you for HIS GLORY and shower Miracle's into your life"!

Bye for now and "May the GOD of the Universe cover you all, lead and guide you all and pour out His Abundant Blessings upon you all, as you remember these Amazing True Testimonies, from The People of Medicine Hat, Alberta, Canada"!!

Remember: GOD is the REWARDER of those that seek HIM! DON'T give up, No Matter what your situation looks like!

Believe and Be Blessed Always, in Jesus Name.

Elizabeth Storres

6 Titles by Lana Kuystermans / Pen Name -
LOTTIE GILLMORE

1: Soft Petal Poems with
HEARTFELT Love

2: Supernatural flying Monkeys
and dancing chickens

3: A Little House on a Great Big Hill

4: A Hat Full of Miracles

5: TRIUMPHANT INNOCENCE

6: Moles Christmas Surprise

All Available at Amazon and major
book stores can be ordered in.
https://www.thriftbooks.com/a/lottie-
gillmore/1762405/

A Hat Full of Miracles-Available
MEDIA LITERARY EXCELLENCE
Book Store online
https://medialiteraryexcellence.com

About the Author

Hello to all my dear friends and family. Well my 4th book is being released and I do believe it will touch the heart of every person that reads it. As you may know, I have been writing since August of 1996 and my journey of writing has proven to be very fruitfull. God has proven to be by my side daily and also with every book written. I don't believe He is done with me yet, Praise God. My husband of 32 years has been a solid rock in my life and writing carreer while our four beautiful children have grown up into caring, wonderful adults. Since 1996, I as well have been given the carreer of being a Nanny/Housekeeper which has been also a total heart fulfillment. Remember: With Jesus in your life, in a personal way, He will make you also soar like an eagle and the recipient of wonders unexpected! Lottie Gillmor